Role Play in the

T

Ted

Role Play in the Early Years

The Teddy Bears' Picnic
and other stories

Jo Boulton and Judith Ackroyd

**Drama Activities
for 3–7 year olds:**

Book 1

David Fulton Publishers

David Fulton Publishers Ltd
The Chiswick Centre, 414 Chiswick High Road, London W4 5TF

www.fultonpublishers.co.uk

First published in Great Britain in 2004 by David Fulton Publishers

10 9 8 7 6 5 4 3 2 1

Note: The right of Jo Boulton and Judith Ackroyd to be identified as the authors of this work has been asserted by them in accordance with the Copyright, Designs and Patents Act 1988.

David Fulton Publishers is a division of Granada Learning Limited, part of ITV plc.

Copyright © Jo Boulton and Judith Ackroyd 2004

British Library Cataloguing in Publication Data
A catalogue record for this book is available from the British Library.

ISBN 1-84312-123-9

Typeset by FiSH Books, London
Printed and bound in Great Britain

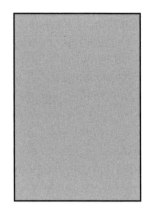

Contents

*For our parents
Anne and Charles
Jean and Derek*

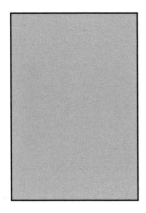

Acknowledgements

We would like to thank the students and teachers who have tried out these materials. We are especially grateful to Sarah Hudson, Georgina Healy and Val Atkins for their stories from the classroom. The support and friendship of colleagues in Education and Performance Studies at University College Northampton is valued and appreciated.

Over the years the work of Dorothy Heathcote, Gavin Bolton, Cecily O'Neill, David Davis and Jonothan Neelands has influenced our practice. We are grateful for their pioneering contributions to the field and their inspiration. Warm thanks to David Booth for his contagious enthusiasm for children's stories.

Thanks are also due to Nina Stibbe at David Fulton Publishers for asking us to write this series. We appreciate the enthusiasm and careful attention of Nina, Paul and Alan throughout the process.

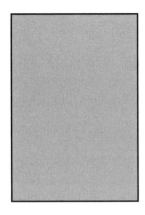

Introduction

*'There's something empowering for young children about drama.
It's about learning and problem-solving in their world.'*

We share teacher Angie Matthews' enthusiasm about using drama with young children and have therefore designed this series of three books to encourage a wider use of drama in the early years settings. The series is designed to support those unfamiliar with drama activity as well as to offer experienced teachers a range of new materials.

Many teachers feel anxious about doing drama, but the fact is that teaching drama can no longer be avoided, no matter how scary it may seem. All children have a statutory entitlement to engage in dramatic activity. Drama is featured in the *Curriculum Guidance for the Foundation Stage* where children are required, for example, to 'Use language to imagine and re-create roles and experiences' (DfEE/QCA 2000: 58). Similarly, in the National Curriculum, at Key Stage 1, drama activities are highlighted. For example, pupils must learn to:

● use language and actions to explore and convey situations, characters and emotions;

● create and sustain roles individually and when working with others;

● comment constructively on drama they have watched or in which they have taken part.

(DfEE/QCA 2000: 44)

The *National Literacy Strategy Framework for Teaching* makes explicit reference to drama. In Year 1, Term 1, for example, children will 're-enact stories in a variety of ways', e.g. 'through role play, using dolls or puppets' (DfEE 1998: 20). Indeed, drama is an interactive and exciting teaching strategy which, by its very nature, illuminates the possibilities for inter-relating the three language modes of speaking and listening, reading and writing.

While drama offers contexts and possibilities for development in aspects of English, it also provides a plethora of other learning opportunities at the same time. So while children are using persuasive language they may also be considering the fragility of the environment. In addition, they may also be developing skills in group work and citizenship all at the same time – through involvement in the same one dramatic activity!

Many teachers are expected to use drama activities with little or no relevant training, often resulting in a lack of both confidence in and understanding of educational drama practice. Student teachers, early years practitioners in Foundation Stage settings and teachers in Key Stage 1 classrooms have regularly asked us for drama ideas they can try with their children that will work. The dramas in this series have been tried and tested by teachers new to drama and also by experienced practitioners. They have found these activities valuable in themselves and also useful as a springboard for developing their own ideas.

There is no doubt that early years practitioners recognise the pedagogic value of children's play. Home corners, imaginative play areas, pretend corners (call them what you will) have been a regular and exciting feature of the early years setting. There are a number of texts available offering ideas and advice on setting up such environments. The activities offered in this series, however, focus on ways that the adult can work in role alongside the children to enhance learning opportunities. Teacher involvement is crucial.

Here it is not just the children who enter imaginative worlds but the children and their teacher who create and explore these fictional worlds together. This approach, namely the teacher in role, enables the teacher to work with the children from inside the drama. The teacher in role can structure the children's contributions, provide stimulating challenges and create appropriate atmospheres. The teacher in role creates situations that demand of the children particular language skills, understanding and empathy. The teacher in role provides a model of commitment to working in role that children can follow.

This book contains a range of drama teaching ideas organised in chapters. In each chapter two types of activity are presented. The drama activities and non-drama activities, such as reading or music are presented in circles. The layout of the activities offers practitioners the possibility of finding their own pathways through the material which are appropriate to their own teaching context. This flexible approach enables pathways through the materials to be selected according to a range of possible factors: the chosen learning objectives; knowledge of the children's needs; the space and time available; the level of teacher confidence; and perhaps the time of year or geographical locality or local events. The three teachers' stories of 'The Teddy Bears' Picnic', a drama from this book, demonstrate how they found their own pathways and different emphases. General aims for the chapters are provided, along with suggestions for resources. Each drama activity indicates possible teacher intentions to make clear the dramatic process. The relevance of each of the dramas to the National Curriculum and Early Learning Goals is set out at the end of the book.

Since this is the first book in the series, we have included the transcript of a teaching session of 'The Park' which is Chapter 8 in this book. This is not to invite you to replicate the way it was done in this instance, but to give you an idea of how drama occurs in the classroom as opposed to how it appears in a book. It illustrates how a teacher can respond to what the children bring and to the moments when they do not contribute. It is an honest, straightforward account of a drama teaching experience with the words of both teacher and children.

The following chapters will help teachers to create a range of imaginary contexts in which children will encounter weird and wonderful, noble and naïve, wicked and whimsical characters.

Sarah Hudson taught her first drama lesson using one of these chapters. She writes:

Without wanting to sound too nauseating and over the top, I would say that this afternoon was one of the most rewarding I have had the pleasure of sharing with my pupils. It has definitely inspired me to continue drama activities with my class. If a novice, or a non-expert, could manage this with such success, then I am sure that anyone could.

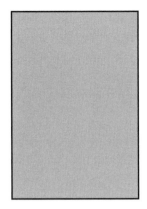

How to use this book

Where do I begin if I have never done drama before?

Looking at 'The Teddy Bears' Picnic' (Chapter 1) and then at 'Stories from the classroom' will give you a sense of how these dramas work and what is required of you. You can also read the transcript of 'The Park' drama to get a feel of what might take place.

It is probably best to follow the activities step by step when you begin using drama. You will soon want to add your own ideas.

Do the dramas fulfil any National Curriculum objectives or Early Learning Goals?

Yes. All the dramas provide the possibility of covering a very wide range of Early Learning Goals (ELGs) and National Curriculum (NC) objectives, as you will see at the back of the book. You may choose to focus on specific objectives which may be most appropriate to your children and their needs.

How many children do I work with?

These dramas have been designed for use with any number of children between groups of four and thirty.

How long do the dramas take?

You need to consider how long you have and how long you wish to give to the activities. We recommend a maximum of thirty minutes with children in the Foundation Stage. However, we have sometimes lost track of time and found that we have been working for much longer. You need to gauge the children's response.

You may choose to teach just one activity and then pick up the story again another time. You can do a drama in one session or over a week.

What initial information is provided?

- Each chapter is laid out with an introduction telling the story of the drama.
- The overall aims of the drama are then provided which concern both drama and other curriculum areas.
- Key themes are listed.

- Resources are listed. These are usually optional, but any essential items are indicated. Some resources have been included, such as the words to 'The Teddy Bears' Picnic' song.
- Also provided are suggestions for imaginative play areas.

How are the activities explained?

- Drama and non-drama activities are provided. The non-drama activities are presented in circles at the side of the page.
- Teacher's intentions for each activity are listed. These pertain to the thinking behind the particular activity described. Headings provide an indication of both the type of dramatic activity (e.g. 'Whole-group improvisation') and the content (e.g. 'Waking the teddies').
- *Italics* are used to distinguish direct speech from explanation. The direct speech provides suggestions of what the teacher might say and examples of what children have said during the drama.
- Clear explanations of drama terminology used in the chapters are included in the Glossary of Terms.

Do I have to follow the plan?

No! It is important that you read through the materials to familiarise yourself with the story. You can then make choices about your own pathway through the materials. In 'Stories from the classroom' we see that Sarah decided not to sing 'The Teddy Bears' Picnic' song, but chose to spend longer matching the teddies with the children's individual needs. Val, however, chose to include a journey in this drama, which she used as a stimulus for a writing activity. The plans can be followed as they are laid out, or you can select which activities you wish to use depending on your experience, your context and your children. You can make the dramas your own as Sarah, Val and Georgina have done.

Do I have to use teacher in role?

Yes. All of these dramas include teacher in role to some degree. The rationale behind this series of books is based upon the teacher working in role from inside the fiction alongside the children. However, this does not mean that you have to use exaggerated voices and walks. You are not required to wear a costume or use props, although we provide suggestions of what might be used to help young children distinguish between you as teacher and you in role. It is important that you make it very clear when you are in role to avoid confusion. A hat is often easy to take on and off as you move between teacher and role.

How do I use an imaginative play area?

Imaginative play areas can be set up by the teacher and children together. They provide a context for the dramas. This does not mean to say that you have to do the drama in the imaginative play area. If you are working with a large group, there won't be room. In this case, you can refer to the imaginative play area as if it is your backdrop.

Suggestions for how you might create such areas are provided in the chapters.

All of the dramas can be taught without imaginative play areas. If you are working in a large space, such as a school hall, we strongly recommend that a corner is cordoned off because too much space can lead to difficulties.

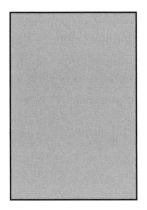

Stories from the classroom

The Teddy Bears' Picnic

We asked three local teachers to write stories about their experiences of using 'The Teddy Bears' Picnic' (Chapter 1) with their classes. Sarah is an art specialist and had not had experience of using teacher in role before. Val has taught for twenty-eight years and, although she has not been trained in drama, she has used our lesson plans over the years. Georgina involves herself in drama both in school and out, and has used teacher in role before.

Reading their stories may help you to conceptualise how the teaching materials are transported from page to practice. The children's names have been changed.

Sarah Hudson's story
Falconer's Hill Infant School, Daventry, Northamptonshire

After a dusty teddy hunt looking for bears under my children's beds and asking colleagues in school, I finally amassed a varied troop of twenty-four bears including several cuddly toy dogs, rabbits and cats – all close friends of the bears of course. They only just fitted into two large plastic boxes, and I needed a full-size blanket to cover them all snugly (so much for covering them with a tea-towel!).

The children arrived in the classroom after lunch and were keen to know what was under the blanket. Register was completed in record time, as the children were so eager to find out what was under the covers. They were all able to keep quiet so as not to wake the teddies and loved reminding me when I forgot.

The children entered into helping me out of my dilemma, namely not knowing what to do on a teddy bears' picnic, with much care and thought. They gave ideas of games we could play. I had to lead them round to the theme of food and drink, but once they got started, this brought forth many ideas. Most of the children created imaginative and extravagant offerings for the magic picnic bag. I noticed that some of the less able children repeated what the previous child had offered but they still felt they had contributed something. Mark offered a cake, as Sandeep had done before him. My questioning about Sandeep's cake had revealed a chocolate sponge with ice-cream on top. To value Mark's contribution, I started by saying, 'You clever boy! I think you have made one of the teddies' favourite cakes! Can I smell some strawberries in it?' Mark was delighted to find that he had made such a popular cake, and his teddy chose him because he knew Mark had made him such a delicious cake.

This boost to the children's self-esteem continued all afternoon, as the part of the drama where the bears chose their child was so powerful and moving. I know the experience will stay with the children and with me for a long time. When the most beautiful large bear with a dolphin necklace round her neck chose Nikki, a small, shy girl lacking in confidence, she grew in stature and her face showed the joy and amazement she felt at being picked by the most wonderful of all the bears. David, a large, active and popular boy, who often finds sitting listening very difficult, was also pleased when a small, tatty bear chose him because he knew that David would help him to be a good listener. Because I knew the class well this allowed me to match all the children to the bears in this individual way that would challenge them.

I found it a moving experience to watch these small children look after the bears in such a loving way. Children such as Christian, who often finds it very difficult to play co-operatively, held his bear in a careful and gentle way and kissed him tenderly before putting him back in the basket.

Without wanting to sound too nauseating and over the top, I would say that this after-noon was one of the most rewarding I have had the pleasure of sharing with my pupils. It has definitely inspired me to continue drama activities with my class. If a novice, or definitely a non-expert, could manage this with such success, then I am sure that anyone could.

I teach in a team of three parallel classes and we always plan collaboratively, so as usual we all planned this drama activity on consecutive days so that the troop of bears could be shared. My colleague, Belinda Dugdale, has been teaching for many years and is a very experienced teacher. My other colleague, Adele Hammond, is enjoying her first year teaching. Although we planned the teddy drama together, it was fascinating how our experiences of the sessions varied, since we had allowed the drama to unfold in a way that was responsive to our indi-vidual classes.

Belinda gave each teddy a name and this entranced the children. During her picnic the children and bears played hide-and-seek and then, when she asked the children to come and sit down, she discovered that Bobby's teddy had played the game so well that he was really lost. Poor Bobby was so worried that some of the other children and bears had to go and search for him. The children entered into the drama so completely that they found him behind a willow tree. He was really wedged under a stool in the book corner. Bobby hugged the bear and the whole class breathed a sigh of relief.

Adele's drama session was timetabled to follow both the other classes, and a little girl, Louise, said to Adele at the beginning of the drama, 'Ah, here they are. I wondered when the teddies were going to visit us.' Word had obviously spread around the playground that the teddies were coming. Adele was pleased that the children used such rich, descriptive language when offering their food for the picnic and she felt this could be a good shared experience on which to base some writing, since the children had enjoyed such a stimulat-ing experience.

▌ Val Atkins' story
▌ Grendon Primary School, Grendon, Northamptonshire

I was happy to do 'The Teddy Bears' Picnic' as I have done drama before with lots of success. However, I have always done it with smaller groups of Year 1 children. This is the first time I have involved reception children. The only thing that concerned me was work-ing with a large group of children who had not experienced teddy drama with me before. A few of them are very quiet and lack confidence in a large group, whereas many others find it diffi-cult to sit and concentrate. Some of the Year 1 boys would have preferred to do something involving bombs and the hulk! Not an easy class! I began the drama by setting some ground rules. They listened carefully when I told them that when I was wearing my glasses and a hat I would be a different person. I explained that they would need to use lots of imagination. I asked them to tell me what they understood by 'imagination' and a popular explanation was 'things in pictures'.

I chose to use the drama as a stimulus for some unaided writing with the Year 1 children, so I wanted them to have as many mental images as possible and to be able to retell the story in sequence. The drama proceeded, and most of the children were very excited and animated when giving me the instructions for how to arrange a picnic. I found it difficult to engage a few of the children who wouldn't speak. Other children tried to whisper to them during this time and I felt I did begin to lose the attention of some of the younger children. The children responded well to being quiet because the teddies were asleep, and were keen to look under the blanket. I chose to distribute the teddies, giving them names and making up stories about them. I think I could have made more out of this and involved the children in questioning and discussion about the bears.

As we continued our journey I encouraged the children to visualise where we were going – 'across the field, up the hill, down the path, past the lake, mind the stinging nettles!' – so that they could use the reverse procedure on the way back. This was a success and helped when the children were following up by drawing pictures. The session was a success and proved that 'The Teddy Bears' Picnic' is a good starting point for drama. It was great fun!

Georgina Healy's story
Danesholme Infant School, Corby, Northamptonshire

The children I work with are in the Foundation Stage, so most are 4 years old. They are not yet full time; therefore there was just a half class to do the drama. The children had had some drama experience, but this had centred on physically joining in with stories. A significant minority of the children has speech problems and although they are willing to make verbal contributions they can be very difficult to understand. All the children had experienced teddy bears and saw them as comforting and non-threatening.

All the children were involved with the story and the group's involvement level was high. Through their responses they showed understanding and empathy. The children could access the activities as they were going from the familiar into strange territory at a gentle pace. Their involvement with the drama was maintained throughout, which is unusual with very young children, who often flick their attention from one thing to another quickly. They were definitely transformed from their everyday selves through this work. They were willing to speak and act in role. The structure of the drama allowed the non-verbal children to communicate using gesture and expression. They particularly enjoyed identifying with the bears. The world they entered was positive, with them in control of the momentum and direction of the story development.

I introduced an additional personal prop: a very big teddy. This elicited responses from the children, but I would not use such a large prop again since it served to be a distraction! The children's attention was drawn to the large teddy, so it worked against their developing involvement. The teddy was removed by me and placed on an adult chair to 'watch the story'. Both teacher and children soon forgot the teddy.

The story matched the children's everyday experiences, creating a secure starting point for them. The plan was structured which allowed for pace and direction, but it was not so prescriptive as to exclude the stamp of personal development. I will use the plan again to enhance future work to be completed on stories, and I feel confident about sharing the plan with teachers who do not usually use drama as a teaching tool. The plan did allow for all sorts of contributions that included and valued the children. I felt that the drama could easily be extended to cover more than one session. It certainly left the children wanting to do more.

I did not find that the children had difficulty accessing the piece and we spent forty-five minutes on it. This is a long time to spend on one thing, but the children were running with it! To create the same pace of development in a full class of thirty very young children I think I would divide the plan into sections and teach for shorter periods. The structure and content of the plans allowed the children to maintain being in role and it moved the majority on from the 'show me' type of characterisation.

After we had done the drama, I put the teddies into the book corner just to observe the interaction the children might have with them. I observed the group who had done the drama as well as the other group who had not. The children who had done the drama went far more into fantasy with the bears. They included them with what they were doing in the book corner. The children who had not done the drama either ignored them or gave them a cursory cuddle.

Perhaps most exciting for me when teaching this drama was the face of one child who has been found difficult in school and who has not yet integrated with the other children. His face was a picture. Pure concentration. He really cared!

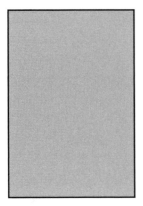

The Park:
Transcript of a lesson

Since this is the first book in the series, we have included the transcript of an activity in 'The Park' drama (Chapter 8). This is not to invite you to replicate the way it was done in this instance, but to give you an idea of how drama occurs in the classroom as opposed to how it appears in a book. It illustrates how a teacher can respond to what the children bring and to the moments when they do not contribute. It is an honest, straightforward account of a drama teaching experience with the words of both teacher and children.

Flower Park: meeting Tariq

[Started with a slow, reassuring discussion.]

Teacher:	We've built a really beautiful park here. Would you like to do some drama about your park today?
All:	Yes!
Teacher:	Why did we decide to call it Flower Park?
Gemma:	Because it's pretty. There's lots of flowers and stuff in it.
Teacher:	It's certainly pretty. Could someone tell me some of the things we can find in Flower Park?

[Wrote a list to help build belief and investment.]

All:	Swings; roundabouts; see-saw; slide; climbing frame; swimming pool; trees; bench; sand-pit; duck pond; clouds; grass; flowerpots with flowers; sun; café . . . .
Teacher:	Why do we have a bench in our park?
Sarah:	'Cos you might get tired and if you're hurt you might want a little rest.
Dean:	You could sleep on the bench.
Teacher:	Yes. That's a good idea. Has anybody been to Flower Park recently? What sort of things do you like to do there?
Abigail:	I play with my friends.
Carrie:	I go to the café to eat something.
Teacher:	What things do you like to eat?
Carrie:	Burgers, beans and chips.
Teacher:	Oh, they sell that sort of food in the café do they? Who else goes to Flower Park?

Lee:	I go on the slide and I play.
Teacher:	Have you ever been to Flower Park, Michael?
Michael:	Yes. I look after the swimming pool.

[Michael chooses his own role.]

Teacher:	Do you? Why is that then?
Michael:	It's my job.
Teacher:	That's a very good job. Has anyone been swimming there? What's it like to swim there?
Terry:	Warm. I chucked my football in the water.
Teacher:	That sounds like a good game.
Terry:	I go with my sister.
Leon:	I go to the duck pond.

[Leon doesn't often speak in large groups so I must encourage him.]

Teacher:	What did you do at the duck pond?
Leon:	I throw things.
Teacher:	What sort of things do you throw?
Leon:	Bread and stuff.
Teacher:	You threw some bread to the ducks. How many are there?
Leon:	Five. No, seven.

[Dean is messing about. I must draw him into the drama.]

Teacher:	What did you do in Flower Park, Dean?
Dean:	I went on the water on a speedboat.
Leon:	Boats on the pond. Not speedboats.
Teacher:	I've learnt quite a few things that I didn't know before. Now I've got something to show you.

[I move on the drama and increase the tension by placing a large bag in the middle of the circle.]

| Michael: | What is it? |

[The bag is injecting interest and provoking curiosity.]

| Teacher: | What do you think is in this bag? |
| All: | Clothes; presents; paper. |

[Clothes are taken from the bag. The children are invited to come forward and take one item out and describe it. The items of clothing provide a new focus for the drama.]

Ben:	A hat. It's smart. It's got a green band.
Riva:	An old coat...it's dirty.
Leona:	Trousers and boots.

Teacher:	And a broom to go with all the clothes. What type of person do you think these clothes belong to?
All:	A sweeper man; a dustman; my dad.
Teacher:	Would you have a dustman in Flower Park do you think?
Sarah:	Yes. If there's rubbish.
Michael:	It could be the keeper man who looks after the park.
Teacher:	Would you like to meet the person who owns these things? He is going to come to the Flower Park.
Dean:	Yes. It can't be you. You've got a skirt on.
Michael:	Yes, it is you. You sweep out the swimming pool for me.

[I begin to dress in the clothes. I ask the children to help me put on the coat and button it up. My movements become slower and more deliberate. I'm not speaking but my body is becoming gradually more bent. I am in role now and provide a focus.]

Tariq:	Oh dear. Oh dear me. My poor back.
Gemma:	Oh dear.

[I am pulling on the wellington boots with great difficulty and am beginning to slowly build up the role. The atmosphere is tense. I can sense their concern. I must remain clear about the effect I want the role to create.]

Carrie:	Do they fit?
Tariq:	Well I'm afraid they're a bit tight on the old feet really. Thank you for asking.

[I'm looking around nervously. I try to sound confident.]

Tariq:	Hello everybody. Hello, I'm Tariq. I'm the park keeper here. I haven't seen any of you before because I'm new.

[I'm trying to sound proud and hold on tightly to the broom.]

Tariq:	I've got a new job. I'm looking after this park. Does anyone know what the park is called?
All:	Flower Park.
Michael:	And I'm the owner of the swimming pool.

[He's asserting his role now. I wonder whether others will follow?]

Tariq:	Oh, I'm very pleased to meet you. Excuse me everybody, do you mind if I have a sit down with you for a little while?
Gemma:	Sit there.
Tariq:	On this bench? It's my back you see. I shouldn't really have this job 'cos of me back.
Michael:	I'll do it for you.
Tariq:	Well, that will be very helpful, but first can I have a chat with you 'cos I don't meet many people. Can you sit down 'cos it makes me a bit nervous if you're all standing up.

Gemma:	Come on, sit down everyone.
Tariq:	Well, my name's Tariq and as I said I haven't been a park keeper before. They said I had the right clothes, but I don't know why really.
Michael:	Your clothes are dirty.
Tariq:	Is it a dirty job being a park keeper?
David:	Yes. You get mud on you when it rains.
Sarah:	There's lots of mud and dirt here.

[I start sighing deeply. I want them to make the next move and offer some suggestions.]

Tariq:	Well, I don't really know what I have to do to be a park keeper.
All:	Sweep paths; pick up paper; tidy up . . . .
Kirsty:	That's what the gloves are for, so your hands don't get germs.
Gemma:	I've already been tidying up the mess.
Tariq:	That's very kind. Could you show me what I have to do? There are some brooms over there.

[I indicate a pile of imaginary brooms. I'm trying to put demands on them. The children pick them up. General movement, sweeping and chatter.]

| Tariq: | I've got a list of things to do somewhere. |

[I search my pockets.]

| Gemma: | Here it is, it's fallen out. |

[She picks up a scrap of imaginary paper and hands it to Tariq.]

Tariq:	Oh dear. I can't read it. What does it say?
Gemma:	Sweep the paths.
Tariq:	OK, we'd better get sweeping. This is hard work. I'm sweating.

[This is getting them up and moving, and also building belief in the park and their roles. Lots of general action. Finding lost toys and shoes. Tariq takes off his hat as a signal that teacher is talking and the drama has stopped. Everyone gathers round. I want to reflect on what has happened so far. Also to slow down the pace again and recap.]

Teacher:	What sort of man is Tariq?
Carrie:	He's the sweeper.
Abigail:	He's the park keeper, he's new.
Teacher:	Is there anything you'd like to know about Tariq?
Abigail:	Yes. How he looks after the park.
Teacher:	Perhaps you can ask him some questions?

[I replace the hat.]

| Tariq: | Thank you ever so much for helping me. I've never seen so much litter. |
| Michael: | Every morning we'll help you clean up. |

Tariq: That's kind. Thank you.

Abigail: How will you look after the park?

Tariq: Well, I've got my list.

Gemma: You've got bad eyesight. I'll read it. 'Everyone will help Tariq to tidy up, clear up and get rid of the rubbish. Collect toys and lost property.'

Michael: We've done that.

Gemma: We can go in the café for a tea-break.

Tariq: Perhaps someone who works in the café could bring us out some coffee?

[Six children go, fetch some drinks and hand them round. This again helps to build belief in their roles.]

Michael: I'll go and open up the swimming pool now.

Sarah: I'll go and dry the slide.

Jody: I'll go and open up the café.

[The children disperse and become involved in dramatic play. Tariq wanders around chatting and asking questions. Michael is creating his own story now.]

Michael: Excuse me, I've got a problem. The swimming pool is frozen so we can't open up today.

Tariq: What are we going to do now?

Michael: Pour hot water on it, then put up a notice to say it's closed.

Dean: We'll sort it out.

Michael: Will you write a sign? Say, 'Sorry everyone, pool is frozen.'

Kirsty: I've just found a hedgehog.

[I feel the drama is losing focus now and need to inject some direction and tension.]

Tariq: Excuse me, the phone's ringing. *[I pick up an imaginary telephone.]* It's Mr Johnson from the council.

Michael: Tell him the pool's frozen.

Tariq: I'm afraid the pool's frozen. Yes. OK. Oh dear. Goodbye. Mr Johnson says it's not good enough. He says the park isn't pretty enough to be called Flower Park.

Kirsty: We'll plant more flowers and seeds.

Tariq: Do you know how to plant seeds?

[Tariq shows his ignorance and allows them to share their knowledge.]

All: Yes.

Tariq: Can you show me?

Abigail: You dig a hole and then put the seed in, cover it up, then put water on it.

Tariq: What sort of seeds should we grow?

All: Daffodils; tulips; cress . . . .

Abigail: Let me phone him. *[Phones.]*

[I'm pleased she's using the drama strategy I have introduced.]

Abigail:	He says yes. I've got some packets in my pocket.
Michael:	Put them round the swimming pool.
Tariq:	Have you got spades here?

[Seeds are planted. Dramatic play. Teacher asks them to sit down.]

Teacher:	Tariq has gone now.
All:	Ahhh.
Daniel:	You were Tariq.
Teacher:	Yes I was. Has anyone got anything to say about Tariq?
Gemma:	He was a very nice man.
Teacher:	What did you think of him when you first met him?

[I want them to see the role of Tariq as someone distinct from me, their teacher.]

Gemma:	Sad. He had a bad back.
Abigail:	He said 'Please will you help me?'
Jody:	Tariq can come to my house. I'll be his friend.
Teacher:	How old was Tariq?
Carrie:	Old. Very old man.
Gemma:	He was worried about his back.
Dean:	He couldn't clean the park.
Michael:	He was on his own. I looked after the swimming pool for him.
Daniel:	I liked him.
Sarah:	I helped him.
Gemma:	I read the letter for him 'cos he had bad eyesight. He couldn't read very well.
Sarah:	Can we play with Tariq another day?
Teacher:	Another day. Yes.

[This process of reflecting on the drama helps the children to remember events and also to sort out their feelings. They begin to understand who Tariq was and what they did to help him. The children worked together to make a story about Tariq in the park and met the challenge he posed.]

CHAPTER 1

The Teddy Bears' Picnic

It doesn't seem to be a very good day for the teddy minder. The teddies, now asleep in a basket, hadn't wanted to have their afternoon nap so she had promised that when they awoke, she would take them on a teddy bears' picnic. The trouble is that she isn't sure what you do on a teddy bears' picnic. The children offer her advice about the games to play and songs to sing. They make a picnic of all the things they think the teddies will like to eat and drink. They then join the picnic and look after the teddies until they are tired and ready for bed.

The need to speak quietly so as not to wake the sleeping teddies means that all the children whisper. It is a useful control during discussion, because only one person can be heard at a time. The teacher in role can sometimes appear excited by a child's idea and exclaim loudly and then, putting a hand over her mouth, indicate that she had stupidly forgotten that she must keep quiet.

Aims

- To help children learn the significance of ordering instructions.
- To encourage a sense of responsibility for others.
- To give children an experience of helping an adult.
- To develop vocabulary.

Themes

- Helping others.
- Food.
- Giving advice.

Resources

- A large container or a basket – a plastic washing basket is ideal.
- A tea-cloth to cover the teddies in the basket.
- As many teddies/soft toys as there are children in the group – or enough for them to share.
- *Optional*: paper cut into shapes of food that children can colour in (e.g. banana, burger in a bun, orange, honey jar).
- *Optional*: props for a shop and a kitchen.
- *Optional*: paper cut into teddy bear shapes to be decorated/coloured in.

Notes

When the teddy bears are given out to the children, there is the chance to create specific individual traits in the bears that may be appropriate for particular children. Perhaps a child who can get a little over-excited could be given a bear *who easily gets anxious. He's a fun bear but needs to feel cared for.* A child with low self-esteem and status with peers might be apparently pointed out by the biggest bear in the basket. *Did you say you have seen someone who you would like to be with?* Teddy is whispering in your ear. *All the children here are nice children. Pardon? There is someone special for you, is there? Would you like to point out who you mean?* Move the bear's arm to indicate the child. It gives the child an ego boost and presents him with a positive – indeed, enviable – image in front of the other children.

The imaginative play area can be designed as a kitchen where food for the picnic is made.

'The Teddy Bears' Picnic' by Charlie

Resource

The song sung by Bing Crosby can be heard from the website:
http://members.tripod.com/~sunbear_2/

THE TEDDY BEARS' PICNIC

If you go down in the woods today
You're sure of a big surprise.
If you go down in the woods today
You'd better go in disguise.
For every bear that ever there was
Will gather there for certain, because
Today's the day the teddy bears have their picnic.

Every teddy bear who's been good
Is sure of a treat today.
There's lots of marvellous things to eat
And wonderful games to play.
Beneath the trees, where nobody sees,
They'll hide and seek as long as they please.
'Cos that's the way the teddy bears have their picnic.

If you go down in the woods today
You'd better not go alone.
It's lovely down in the woods today
But safer to stay at home.
For every bear that ever there was
Will gather there for certain, because
Today's the day the teddy bears have their picnic.

Picnic time for teddy bears,
The little teddy bears are having a lovely time today.
Watch them, catch them unawares,
And see them picnic on their holiday.
See them gaily gather 'bout,
They love to play and shout
They never have any cares.
At six o'clock their mummies and daddies
Will take them home to bed
Because they're tired little teddy bears.

Activity 1   Meeting the teddy minder

Teacher's intentions

- To introduce the problem to be solved.
- To give children the experience of being the experts.
- To develop sensitive communication and volume control.

Teacher in role: setting the scene

Enter the space carefully carrying the basket. It is full of teddy bears concealed by the tea-cloth laid over the top. Very carefully, and with great concentration, place it in the centre of the circle. Whisper:

Ssshh. All the teddies are having a sleep. Poor little things. They were so excited about this and now they are going to be so sad when they wake up and find out. I feel very upset about it.

The children may ask what is wrong at this point.

The teddy bears had not wanted to go to sleep, so I stupidly said that if they settled down for their after-lunch sleep, I would take them for a teddy bears' picnic. The trouble is that I don't know what teddy bears do at a teddy bears' picnic. Oh dear. They will be so upset.

Discussion in role: children advise

The children will often offer advice themselves, but if not they can be asked if they can help or if they know anything about teddy bears' picnics.

- *What do they play?*
- *Where do they go for the picnic?*
- *What do they eat?*
- *Isn't there a special song? Something about going down in the woods today... .*

It is important that the teacher in role continues asking questions as the children explain, encouraging them to clarify their explanations and ordering the explanations appropriately.

- *Sandwiches! But I don't know what to put inside the sandwiches. What might they like?*
- *How do you play hide-and-seek?*
- *For how long does the person shut their eyes?*
- *If I am hiding, how do I know when you are coming to look for me?*
- *But what goes after 'ring-a-ring of roses'?*
- *Oh that sounds wonderful! Will you teach me the song?*

Party games

Play hide-and-seek, ring-a-ring of roses, and other games that children suggest.

Shared writing: instructions

A set of instructions for playing a party game.

Rhymes and stories about teddies

Activity 2   Picnic preparations

Teacher's intentions

- To encourage use of imagination.
- To invite children to bring their own tastes and experiences into the pretend context.
- To practise talk for life, such as talking to a shopkeeper.

Dramatic play: preparing the picnic

Ask the children if they would help prepare the picnic and invite them to come too.

Shall we make the picnic first? We should all get something for the picnic and meet here when the clock strikes 3. I will have a picnic basket here ready.

(Move the teddies to 'somewhere quiet' where the children will not be tempted to touch them.)

Some children like to pretend to make sandwiches through mimed activity, others to go to a pretend shop to buy bottled drinks. Move about the space from being in the kitchen asking one child about the cooking processes to being the shopkeeper who sells bananas to another. The space may be organised so that one end is where the shop is and the other is the kitchen. This may be done with or without any concrete props, such as scales and cookers.

If there is an imaginary play area as a kitchen, it is used here.

Ritual: packing the picnic

Indicate the clock striking 3, saying 'Dong' loudly or using an instrument. The children are asked to sit in a circle. The teacher moves into the circle and mimes opening a huge bag, explaining as she does so: *This is a very special bag. It can hold as much as we want to put in it.*

The children watch as the teacher moves back to the edge of the circle, picks up an imaginary cake, carries it to the centre and places it in the bag with care. As she does so, she announces, for example, *a large creamy chocolate cake with chocolate drops on top.*

Children take it in turns around the circle to pick up the food or drink that they have brought and place it in the bag, announcing what it is. Teacher may ask questions about some of them:

- *How will they eat the jelly?*
- *What flavour are the crisps?*
- *Why did you choose honey for the sandwiches?*

Or provide comments as a way of supporting the child's choice:

- *Ooh! I adore raspberry jam!*
- *Thank goodness you remembered drinks! I had forgotten!*
- *I have heard that teddies adore oranges!*

Preparing party or picnic food
Making fruit jelly perhaps, or sandwiches.

Pictures/ colouring in
- Children draw pictures of the food they will put into the picnic bag.
- Or they colour the pre-prepared food shapes.
- Decorate and name teddy bear shapes.

Design and make
Your own teddy.

Activity 3   Activity preparations

Teacher's intentions

- To encourage an understanding of the need for organisation and planning.
- To introduce the teddies in a sympathetic light to encourage a caring response.

Discussion in role: planning the excursion

Explain that before the teddies wake up you want to be clear about what will happen.

- *What do we do first? Eat or sing or play games?*
- *Which game, then?*

The children agree the order of events and it is reiterated so that the minder understands. She may need prompting.

- *So, it's hide-and-seek and then . . . sorry, which game do we do next?*
- *Oh dear, I am glad that you will be with me because I can't remember when we have the food.*

The children are asked if they would be prepared to look after a teddy each (or in twos or threes). *I know that I am asking you to do a very grown-up job and that you will have to be very gentle with the teddies, but I would be so grateful for your help.*

Whole-group improvisation: waking the teddies

Take the basket to the edge of the circle. Peep under the tea-cloth and whisper that the bears seem to be waking. Very gently and slowly lift the tea-cloth off, which will reveal the teddies and soft toys to the children for the first time.

Select one teddy and gently lift it out of the basket – perhaps telling the children its name and something about it.

- *Now, Andrew Bear is very friendly, but I need someone to look after him who will keep an eye on him when he is having his picnic. He does tend to spill his food down his front.*
- *Here is Woolly. He will sing all day if he can. Who will enjoy singing our special song with Woolly?*

Each teddy is given to a child. The teacher must handle the bears very gently to provide a positive role model of a teddy minder. Each child will usually receive the teddy according to how it is given.

Listening to music/singing

Listen to a recording of the song 'The Teddy Bears' Picnic'.

Singing lullabies

Children can sing the teddies to sleep (e.g. Rock a bye baby).

Design and make

A bed for your teddy.

Activity 4   The Teddy Bears' Picnic

Teacher's intentions

- To develop responsibility for others (albeit teddies in this context).
- To participate in the planned event.
- To put the teddies to bed to complete the cycle of their day.

Dramatic play: the picnic

The plans are carried out as organised by the children. For circle games, each teddy will be between two children, so they will hold the bears' paws.

- *Who will tell the bears what we have planned for them next?*
- *You may need to sing more loudly to help them remember the words.*

The children and bears are asked to sit down for the picnic. Children might be given napkins to use for the bears, or wet wipes could be passed around. They will need to wash/wipe the teddies' paws both before and after their food!

Ritual: teddies' bedtime

After the activities have been carried out, everyone sits in a circle with the children holding the bears.

It has been such a lovely day. Thank you so much for your help. I couldn't have done any of this without all of you. I know the teddies have had a wonderful time.

It is time for them to go to bed now after their busy afternoon. Could you say goodnight to them and then I shall call each of you in turn to put your teddy back into the basket.

One by one the teddies are put into the basket again and finally the tea-cloth is placed over the top 'so they can sleep'.

Storytelling

Children explain about what they did with their bear at the picnic. They might include what it ate, whether it was a messy eater, had washed its hands and which games it had most enjoyed.

Teddy collection

Bring your favourite teddy to school to show. Encourage descriptive vocabulary in teddy introductions.

Activity 5   Plenary

Teacher's intentions

- To evaluate the effectiveness of their actions in the drama

Discussion: considering what has been learned.

- Discuss the events.
- How did they help?
- Retell the story chronologically.

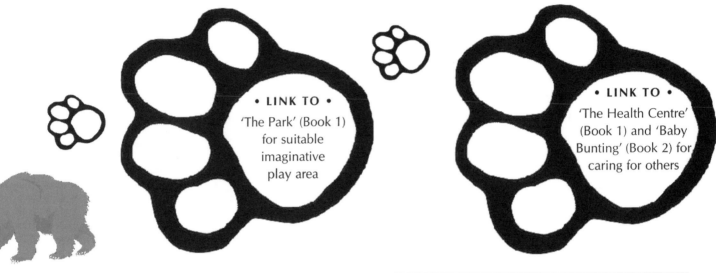

• LINK TO •
'The Park' (Book 1) for suitable imaginative play area

• LINK TO •
'The Health Centre' (Book 1) and 'Baby Bunting' (Book 2) for caring for others

'The Teddy Bears' Picnic' by Grace

CHAPTER 2

The Not-So-Jolly Postman

The children find that the postman, normally a happy, easygoing person, is very sad. He is embarrassed to explain that he is frightened of a dog in the front garden of a house on his round. Ms Woof, who is new in the village, does not understand why anyone could be frightened of her dog and has to be convinced that there is a problem. The children negotiate a resolution, such as the dog being introduced to the postman or it being kept in the back garden in the mornings, rather than in the front. But all this has taken time, and now the postman is afraid that he won't get all the letters delivered on time. The children learn about the addresses he delivers to and help him by delivering the letters themselves through the horizontal and vertical letterboxes.

Aims

- To develop number recognition.
- To encourage reading for a purpose.
- To consider others and their fears.
- To introduce a story-book.
- To invite negotiation and problem-solving.

Themes

- Post delivery.
- Using tact and negotiation.
- Problem-solving.

Resources

- Drawings of doors on large sheets of sugar paper (see p. 25).
- A bag suitable to use as a postal worker's bag.
- Addressed envelopes are required. Children may do these (circle activity p. 26) or they are prepared earlier.
- Addresses displayed on a board for all to read (see p. 24).

The imaginative play area can be designed as a post office.

Resource

Addresses to be displayed

You may wish to use local names so that children become familiar with their shapes and sounds. It is useful to have some familiar words for the names, to enhance recognition and perhaps spelling.

Ms C. Woof 1 Happy Lane Sunlea Northamptonshire	Doctor Pill 2 Happy Lane Sunlea Northamptonshire	Mr R. and Mrs T. Jolly 3 Happy Lane Sunlea Northamptonshire
Miss S. Singh Sun Farm Sunlea Northamptonshire	Mrs J. Wig and Mr E. Ogun Lane End Cottage Sunlea Northamptonshire	Miss O'Casey 4 Happy Lane Sunlea Northamptonshire

The Postman by Charlie

Doors are drawn by the teacher on large sheets of sugar paper in preparation. They should all be slightly different, with either a vertical or horizontal letterbox flap cut into them. Each should also have a number from 1 to 4 or a house name, either 'Sun Farm' or 'Lane End Cottage'. They can be very simple, or more elaborate doors.

Activity 1   The postman's problem

Teacher's intentions

- To develop supportive language.
- To resolve a problem.
- To practise negotiation skills.

Narration: setting the scene

The postman was usually a very jolly postman, but this morning he is not very jolly at all. In fact, he is very sad and hasn't left for his delivery.

Why might he be sad? Guesses are made and ideas are discussed. Invite the children to meet the postman to see if they can find out from him why he is so sad. They can plan what sorts of questions they might ask him.

The teacher explains that when she is on the chair, she will be the postman.

Discussion in role: meeting the postman

The postman looks very glum, twisting the strap of the bag anxiously and looking down. If the children don't speak to him, he may look up and say,

Hello. I am sorry not to be more welcoming to you. He responds very slowly to the children giving the information about his problem:

- *I love my job, but I can't do it anymore . . . .*
- *It is too embarrassing to talk about. . . . You will think that I am stupid . . . .*
- *Someone new has moved into the village . . . I can't deliver there . . . .*
- *My friend got bitten by a tiny dog in the next village . . . and this new dog is huge. It is always in the front garden.*

Children offer to help. The postman has his doubts. The intended conclusion is that the children will wish to go to see Ms Woof, the dog owner. *But what will you say? Why should she take any notice?* The postman does not want to go with them since he is embarrassed (and because the teacher will take the role of Ms Woof!).

Whole-group improvisation: visiting Ms Woof

Agree on where the front gate into Ms Woof's garden is and use a chair to indicate the front of the house. Ms Woof will be washing up by the front window. The children agree among themselves who will speak first and how they will attract Ms Woof's attention. The children will explain the problem as Ms Woof mimes holding a huge dog that may jerk her arm forward from time to time!

Ms Woof responds:

- *You must be mistaken.*
- *No one could be afraid of Giant/Rover/Warrior* [choose a name that implies it's a big tough dog].
- *Maybe the postman is being silly . . . our last postman loved him . . . he is causing trouble without knowing the dog . . . .*

The children will argue the postman's case and Ms Woof can argue on every front. Eventually some solution will need to be reached (e.g. the postman meets the dog, brings it treats, it is tied up for the first few weeks or even in the house or back garden). Flushed with success they go to tell the postman.

This could end the drama, or lead to the next stage.

Activity 2   Delivering the letters

Teacher's intentions

- To develop number identification.
- To encourage reading skills.
- To match words and/or letters.

Discussion in role: the problem of delivering letters

The postman is concerned that he has no time to deliver the letters now that he has wasted so much time over worrying about the dog.

I will get into such trouble if the letters are not delivered on time...there is no way I will get them done now.

Children are always desperate to deliver the letters, but the postman needs to be persuaded.

- *You won't know where all the houses are....*
- *I know about the different letterboxes....*
- *You may put envelopes in the wrong door.*

In the end he is persuaded and shows the children the addresses on a board. They repeat the words on the addresses as he points to them. Some will soon be familiar since they will appear on each envelope, such as the road name and village.

Dramatic play: posting the letters

The teacher gets out the sugar paper doors and pins/sticks the top corners on to the tops of tables around the room, explaining that they will imagine the classroom is the village. The postman opens his bag and passes each child one letter at a time.

The children find the appropriate door to post their envelope into. Some children like to retrieve their letters for the experience of doing it again and re-looking at all the doors as though for the first time.

Whole-class improvisation: talking about the events of the day

The postman invites the children to come for a drink and cake to show his appreciation. As he mimes passing cake around, the children are invited to describe their delivery. Had they seen any dogs? Were any letterboxes awkward? Did they see any friends on their way?

Descriptions
What does your front door look like? What colour is it? Is there a doorknob? Are there any windows in the door? Put your hand up if your letterbox is vertical like this one. Or horizontal? Where else are letters delivered? Does anyone have a mailbox?

Discussion
Talk about different writing scripts used on packages and envelopes (e.g. cursive, printed, handwritten).

Story telling or shared writing
Write or tell another story about the postman.

Activity 3   Plenary

Discussion: considering what has been learned

- What were the postman's problems?
- Do the children know anyone who is afraid of dogs or other animals?
- How will things be different for the postman at Ms Woof's house?
- How did the children bring this about?

Sign-making

Signs saying 'Beware of the Dog' can be made and perhaps illustrated.

Vocabulary extension

- Brainstorm a list of words that mean 'happy' and a list that mean 'sad'.
- Practise making happy and sad faces.
- Read the words aloud in random order. The children make the appropriate expression to check that they remember what all the words mean.

Discussion

How are dogs trained? When are we frightened of dogs? What commands are dogs taught? Who has dogs? What have they been trained to do?

Collect
Stamps or postcards from around the world.

Emergent writing
Children write letters that are then placed in the envelopes. If names are legible on the letters, they are matched with names on the envelopes.

Write letters
To people you know and post them! Wait for the reply.

ICT
Use the floor turtle to deliver letters to different houses on a map.

Learn
Your address!

Design and make
A class post-box.

• LINK TO •
'The Park' (Book 1) and 'The Health Centre' (Book 1) and 'Farmer Roberts' Farm' (Book 2) for jobs in the community

• LINK TO •
'Mary Mary and the Giant' (Book 2) and 'The Lonely Dragon' (Book 3) for fears

CHAPTER 3

The Lost Hat

What started out as a lovely walk, turned out to be a disaster. To have found the most beautiful hat in the world, to wear it out in the park, then only to lose it in a gust of wind, is more than anyone could bear. The children discover that the Man of the Wind has got the hat, and in spite of all they have heard about the anger and temper of this character, they determine to find him and get the hat back. All is not, of course, quite as they expect. The Man of the Wind has also fallen in love with the hat and wants to wear it to a very special hat party. Everyone will laugh at him if he hasn't got a hat on. The children have the task of sorting things out between the owner of the hat and the Man of the Wind.

Aims

- To use different modes of talk.
- To work together to solve problems.
- To develop aspects of citizenship – not judging others by assumptions.

Themes

- Hats.
- Fairness.
- Stealing.
- Saying sorry for mistakes.

Resources

- *Optional*: a cloak for the Man of the Wind.

The imaginative play area can be designed as a hat shop.

The children can make paper folded hats, and paint pictures of hats that can be cut out and mounted as though they are on hat stands.

Activity 1   Discovering the problem

Teacher's intentions

- To introduce the problem.
- To encourage questioning skills.

Discussion in role: children discover information

Explain that you are going to play a very worried person who wants to talk to the class. Ask the class if they will listen to someone who is a bit upset. How will they look at the person as they listen to help her to feel less anxious?

- *Oh, you can't imagine what has just happened.*
- *The most dreadful thing.*
- *I've lost my beautiful new hat.*

Let the children ask for details by providing pauses for them. The general information is as follows, but it may emerge in a different order every time you do it.

- *I had just bought the hat. It was the most beautiful hat I'd ever seen.*
- *What colour do you think the most beautiful hat in the world would be?*
- *Look at one child. Yes! It was just that colour. You see it was the most beautiful hat in the world.*
- *It had a ribbon around it, too.*

Look at someone else. *What colour do you think the ribbon would be on the most beautiful hat in the world?* Again, whatever is said is exactly the colour.

You see how special it was now. I was walking proudly in the park wearing it for the very first time. It was quite a windy day and suddenly a tremendous gust of wind blew it right off my head, and up high into the sky. I watched it blowing out of my reach until I caught the last glimpse of ribbon before it disappeared from sight.

Discussion in role: the challenge

I know the Man of the Wind must have it. I've heard he's taken things before. But I am afraid to go to him on my own.

Children find this an irresistible challenge.

This is very kind of you, but you know how frightening he is; so angry all the time, so wild.

You need the children's advice on how to find him, too.

- *Where do you think he lives?*
- *How will we get there?*
- *How long will it take us?*

Brainstorm 'hats'

Who wears hats? Which hats are worn for safety reasons? Who can we recognise by their hats? What is the biggest/ most silly/colourful hat you have seen? At which special occasions might we wear hats?

Collective drawing

Each child adds detail to a hat to make it 'the most beautiful hat in the world'.

Bringing hats

Children can bring in hats and talk about when they are worn and what they are made of or what they are for. Some may have religious connotations, others may signify a job or leisure activity.

Activity 2   Preparation and journey

Teacher's intentions

- To build belief in roles.
- To encourage imagination and use of descriptive language.

Dramatic play: preparing transport

Whatever form of transport was suggested for the journey needs to be prepared for this special expedition. If a bus, it should be painted so it is clear that this is not an ordinary bus, but a bus with a very special purpose. If it is a rocket, it may need to be built.

The work is carried out through dramatic play. The children pretend to build and the teacher moves around among them with action plans, comments and questions to help build their belief in the task.

- *It'll be hard to reach to paint up there.*
- *Shall I hold the ladder?*
- *What colour will you paint this part?*
- *This is going to be a lucky car, I reckon.*
- *Have you been in a rocket before?*

When the job is finished, everyone should admire the work, making statements about what it looks like and what it feels like to have finished:

- *That's a good job done.*
- *Now we are ready to go.*
- *I think the shiny parts look good.*
- *I hope it will get us there.*

Read hat stories

For example, *The Quangle Wangle's Hat* by Edward Lear, *Ho for a Hat!* by William Jay Smith, *The Extraordinary Hatmaker* by Malcolm Carrick.

Narration and enaction: the journey

Agree where the door is and where the seats are. Narration:

Everyone fell silent. They looked at the rocket/bus/balloon and felt pleased with their work. They formed a line at the door. One at a time they entered the rocket and took a seat.

You may nod at each one as they enter as though you are checking that they should be on the rocket.

They felt excited, but also a bit worried about meeting the Man of the Wind.

If it is a rocket, you need to provide a countdown to lift-off. Explain that as they begin to move, the children will take over they storytelling by describing what they might see through the windows:

- *We're going past the school!*
- *The houses are getting smaller now.*
- *These clouds are like cotton wool.*

Finally, exclaim that you have seen the sign. *We must be there. It says, 'The Man of the Wind's Residence'.* You wonder what residence means . . . .

Guessing hats

The teacher puts a collection of hats into a bag or box. They are brought out one at a time and discussed and tried on. Children may stroll down an imaginary catwalk to show off the hat while someone else describes it.

Activity 3   Meeting the Man of the Wind

Teacher's intentions

- To provide a challenging discussion.
- To encourage negotiation skills.
- To resolve the drama.

Discussion in role: how to approach the Man of the Wind

- *I wouldn't dare go on my own.*
- *What stories have you heard about him?*
- *I heard that he lifted someone's garden shed right up from the garden and threw it into the river nearby!*

The children share stories that they make up. *Should we go in angrily because he has stolen the hat, or carefully because he could be very frightening and maybe even dangerous?*

Strategy is discussed. You explain that you are too frightened to go and that you will wait for them by the gate, *but you will get the hat back for me, won't you. Good luck!*

Design a hat

Each child designs a hat for the Man of the Wind.

Whole-group improvisation: meeting the Man of the Wind

Agree where the imaginary door to his house is. Explain that you will now take the role of the Man of the Wind. You may wish to wear a cloak to indicate the change of role.

The children will approach him as they have planned and will ask questions, perhaps tell him off and request the hat. The Man of the Wind tries to look powerful, but gradually they discover his story:

- *I am not really nasty and I know I shouldn't have taken the hat.*
- *I just thought it looked so lovely. I put it on and felt good wearing it.*
- *I have never seen anything so beautiful before and therefore want to keep the hat.*
- *I am planning to wear it to a party this very evening.*
- *If the children take the hat, I will have nothing nice to wear and people will laugh at me.*

Making hats

Children can make very basic hats by folding paper. The teacher folds the paper, and the children watch and copy with their own paper.

As the children gradually learn these things, they may wish to tell him that he has behaved badly, upset someone and actually taken what isn't his. They may also want to try to help him. They may offer to buy another hat, ask the owner if he can borrow it or make him a new one. They may suggest that he can borrow the hat only if he sends a message to say sorry.

Don't make it too easy for the children to resolve the situation. Be unwilling to part with the hat for a while. You may think more about yourself at the party than of the fact that you have stolen the hat.

The children might be invited to join the party in the end.

Reflection: reporting back to the owner

As the owner of the hat, invite the children to sit down and tell you about what happened:

- *Were you frightened?*
- *Was he a horrid bad man?*
- *What was he like?*
- *Was his house horrid, too?*
- *How did you persuade him to give back the hat?*
- *What did you say to him?*
- *Was he easy to persuade?*

Activity 4   Plenary

Teacher's intentions

- To consider the story and create possible endings.

Discussion: considering what has been learned

- *Who did we meet?*
- *What was the problem?*
- *How do you think the story might end?*

Matching hats

Match the hat with the person who might wear it (e.g. police helmet and police officer).

Decorating hats

Each child decorates a hat, perhaps for a decorating hat competition or for an Easter event.

Name that hat

Children learn the names of hats through matching words and pictures or actual hats (e.g. bowler hat, Stetson, cycle helmet).

Hats as protection

Discuss which hats might keep us dry in the rain. Test them. Which hats will keep us safe from hard objects? Which hats would protect us from the sun?

• LINK TO •

'Goldilocks' and 'Baz the Vandal' (Book 1), 'Pirate Adventure' (Book 2), 'Under the Sea' (Book 2) and 'Finders Keepers' for moral issues

4 The Dirty River

The villagers are devastated when their beautiful river becomes filthy and full of bottles and cans. They cannot understand how it has happened when they are so careful to protect it because they enjoy using it for their recreation, for example swimming and boating.

Everyone knows that the Wise One may be able to help them. The Wise One lives in the wood near the river. She gives the children clues that lead them to follow the path of the river to its source. There they find the problem. A lady is throwing her rubbish into the stream which takes it down the hillside. The stream becomes a river, which takes the rubbish down to the village. The children must explain to the lady why this behaviour is wrong.

Aims

- To develop reading skills.
- To encourage prediction skills.
- To extend vocabulary related to geometric terms.
- To consider waste and its relationship to the environment.

Themes

- Caring for the environment.
- Pollution.
- Rivers.
- Puzzles and riddles.

Resources

- Rhyme written on a large sheet of paper (see p. 38).
- Six puzzle shapes in card (see p. 38).
- Six envelopes.
- Six large sheets of sugar paper (see p. 39).
- *Optional*: a shawl for your role as the Wise One; a box (cardboard will do).

The imaginative play area can be designed as a riverside park.

Resource

Rhyme

The rhyme should ideally be written on a large sheet of sugar paper, rolled up and tied with a ribbon or piece of string.

> To learn what has caused your sorrow
> A journey lies ahead of you.
> You must follow a trail and leave tomorrow.
> I can help you with a clue.
> The trail will take you who knows where?
> Here in puzzles some help you'll find
> In perhaps a circle, perhaps a square,
> Sort out the message with shapes in mind.

Puzzle shapes

The six puzzle shapes are prepared on card by the teacher. Each shape has a clue written on it and is then cut into pieces and put into six envelopes. Some can be cut into puzzles that will be more difficult to complete than others so that teachers can designate the tasks to different ability groups.

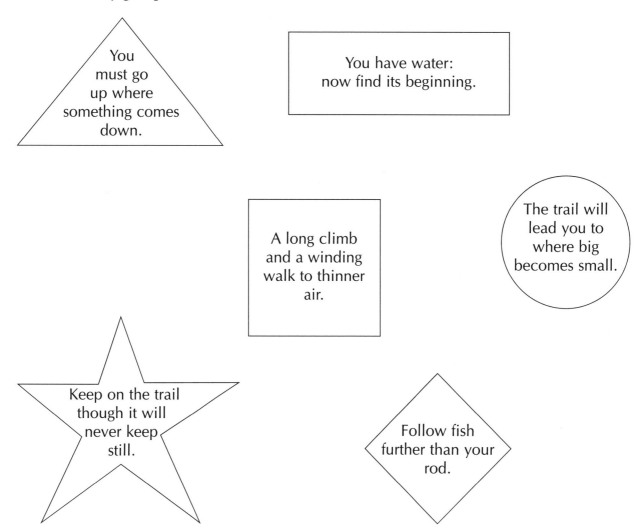

Collective drawings of the river

Large sheets of sugar paper are prepared with the outline of the stream getting wider on each sheet to become a river.

These illustrations are used for the 'Drawing the River' circle activity on p. 43.

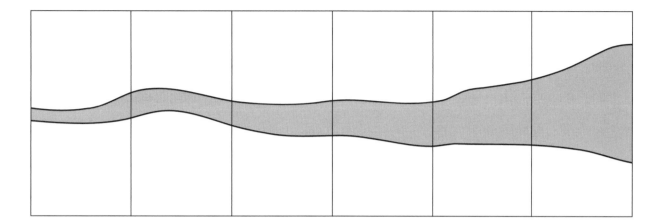

Groups of children work on each sheet to create the environment around the stream/river.

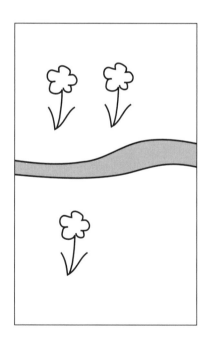
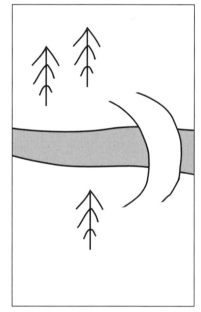

Read stories
Stories involving rivers
and/or pollution.

Activity 1   In a dreamy village far from here

Teacher's intentions

● To set the scene where all is well and in harmony.
● To practise physical control.
● To encourage imaginative ideas and responses to questions posed.

Narration: setting the scene

A long long way from here, where the sun shines nearly every day and the skies are a beautiful blue, there is a village. Through the heart of the village runs a crystal-clear river. Beyond the village are glorious green fields, hills and woodland, but it is down to the river that all the people go in their leisure time. Everyone loves the river and they use it for so many things.

Still image building: creating the community

Discuss what sorts of things the people will do by and on the river. Examples might include swimming, fishing, picnics, water-skiing.

The children make a still image to depict the activities taking place on or by the river. Everyone is a villager doing something. You might agree the whereabouts of the river in the space.

One child at a time steps into the space, while the others stand around the edge. Each child assumes a position depicting a certain activity. The picture is built up so that if one child is water-skiing, another may be driving a speed-boat a little in front as though towing the water-skier.

An option is to invite them to make a statement to describe what they are doing as they pose.

The children can be asked to bring the picture to life for a moment, but must stop and freeze again when the teacher claps. This means that the children can engage in some dramatic play, but are constantly stopping through the teacher's clap control. They must be in control of their bodies to achieve this.

Activity 2   Things fall apart

Teacher's intentions

● To introduce the problem to be solved.
● To encourage the expression of feelings.

Narration: introducing the problem

One morning everything changed. It was a bright morning. Some people had got up early to go to the river to windsurf [or something else that had been depicted in the still image]. When they arrived, they found that the river water looked filthy with rubbish floating in it. One by one the villagers came down to the river and looked at the water in horror. They had taken such good care of the river and wondered what could have happened. They all had something to say about it.

Statementing: it's all gone wrong

The children form two curved lines facing each other as though they are standing on the riverbanks. Each in turn from one side to the other takes a small step forward and makes a statement about their reactions to the discovery.

Examples include *I'm not swimming in that. How did this happen? It's horrid!*

Activity 3   Visiting the Wise One

Teacher's intentions

- To provide a motive to solve geometric puzzles.
- To encourage predictions through the puzzles.
- To name different shapes.

Drawing 2D shapes
Children draw and learn
the names of different
shapes.

Narration: there's someone who can help

Everyone knew what to do. They had heard stories of what the villagers had done when there was a problem back in the past. Some way out [point] across the fields and through the trees is a small clearing. Beneath a large oak tree is a simple wooden seat. They all knew that at some time each day, someone would come to sit on the seat . . . by someone, they meant 'the Wise One'. The Wise One would tell them what they should do. The Wise One had helped their grandparents in the past and would help them now. The villagers made their way across the fields and through the trees. They found the wooden seat, sat down in front of it and waited silently for the Wise One.

Whole-group improvisation: the Wise One's advice

Agree with the class where the wooden seat will be and where they should sit. Place the rolled sugar paper with the rhyme on it in a box or non-transparent bag with the envelopes.

Teacher in role as the Wise One shuffles into the space from behind the seated children hugging the box. She looks intently into the eyes of the villagers, being obsessively protective about the box. She moves between the children making her way to the seat. She speaks mystically.

I knew you'd come. I know those eyes – those sad troubled eyes. I've seen them before. Not in you, but in your grandparents. They came to me here long ago. I helped them and I will help you. Why have you come?

As the children explain, she asks for more details, such as:

- *What colour is the water?*
- *What does it smell like?*
- *When did you first notice the change?*

She looks at individual villagers explaining that she knew they would come and nodding knowingly. She explains that she had seen this trouble in the smoke of her fire last night. She points to one or two pupils.

In my box is a large scroll. It will help you. Get it out. Undo the string and hold it up. Make sure everyone can see it.

The villagers read the rhyme aloud together. They discuss what could be meant by the words.

Finally, the Wise One gets up slowly and says she has something else for them. She grabs the envelopes from the box and waving them emotionally in the air she says in desperation:

Litter collection

In the school grounds or locality.

You will make this journey, won't you? You must sort this out. I am relying on you. When you return and all is well, please come to me and tell me all that took place.

She puts the envelopes down, wishes them luck, and leaves.

Puzzles: where must we go?

Teacher returns to the group as a villager suggesting that the children should work in six groups to see what information they get from what is in the envelopes. As the children work in groups putting the pieces together to form a shape and hence being able to read the clue, move between them:

- *It's a diamond! The rhyme said something about shapes!*
- *What does that mean?*
- *How can we follow a trail that keeps moving?*
- *You've sorted that out quickly, but have you any idea what it means?*

Each group reads their clue to the others and they discuss what the clues mean and try to make connections between them. As a villager, ask specific questions that help comprehension where they get stuck. *Is the air thinner in some places, then? Where? Is it to do with height? Would it be thinner if we were high up or if we are low down in a valley?*

Note: With younger children, the puzzles could be done all together rather than in groups.

Maps and symbols

Look at maps to see how rivers are shown and other water symbols may be identified.

Activity 4 Preparation and journey

Teacher's intentions

- To encourage thinking about implications of a journey.
- To draw upon each child's contribution to a shared endeavour.

Ritual: packing the bag

Teacher narrates to the children sitting in a circle,

The villagers thought hard about the journey ahead of them. None of them had ever travelled out of the village before. One of the villagers had brought a very large bag (teacher moves into the middle of the circle and mimes placing a large imaginary bag and unzipping it).

Each villager placed one item into the bag that they thought would be useful for the journey.

Teacher models the procedure by placing an imaginary rope into the bag saying,

Rope, to help us if we need to climb up rocks.

The children take it in turns to place something in the bag with a statement of what and why.

Looking at pictures

Of different rivers and their environs.

Options: the journey

The journey can be accomplished in a range of different ways. Select one of the following:

If the trail has been drawn, as suggested in the circle activity, the journey should make reference to the features identified.

- Whole-group improvisation: Lead an imaginary journey, talking about it to bring it to life, encouraging the children to climb over imaginary rocks and crawl through thick bushes. No props are required, only imagination and mimed activity. The teacher speaks the journey as the children mime the actions.
- Story circle: Tell the story of the journey around the circle.
- Still images: Create different moments in the story.

Let us all create the moment when we saw the bear. Or ask a few children to get up and illustrate the story as the teacher tells it: *And they had to crawl over the rocks* (indicate three or four children who hold the position until the teacher moves on).

> **Drawing the river**
>
> Use the idea illustrated earlier, of parts of a river drawn on large sheets of paper and completed by the children. These are then placed in a row to show the river getting wider. The children can draw trees and rocks to create the landscape. If they have looked at symbols used on maps, they could use them here.

Activity 5   Discovering the source of the problem

Teacher's intentions

- To bring about a resolution.
- To encourage speaking and listening in a difficult context.

Narration and discussion in role: more clues

Eventually they reached a point high up the mountain where their trail, the river, had become a stream. They were amazed to see a dustbin bag beside the stream near a small house. What a place to see a house! So high! It was certainly the only building for miles. The villagers discussed what they should say to the woman whom they could see in the window of the house.

As a villager, ask the children how they should approach and what they should say, and what sort of voice they should use to get the kind of conversation going so that they can find out what is going on. They prepare their approach.

Whole-group improvisation: meeting the culprit

The woman is very warm and friendly. She is delighted to have visitors and explains that she rarely sees anyone else so high up the mountain, and certainly not such a crowd. *Have you come far? Would you like some tea?*

The children as villagers will talk about why they are there.

> **Vocabulary collection**
>
> Collect words such as pollution, environment, river and stream.

The woman is completely oblivious of causing anyone a problem. She has recently moved from a city where she used to put her bin bags out onto the pavement and a lorry would come and take them away.

I just put my rubbish into my beautiful fast flowing stream and it is taken away. My stream is then beautifully clear again.

When the villagers explain that it is spoiling their river she is confused. This is only a stream and they are talking about a river. Also they live so far away, so it cannot be her rubbish. She has never considered where the rubbish goes, assuming that it has somehow simply disappeared.

As the truth dawns on her, she asks what the river looks like now and what they use it for. She is apologetic and offers to return to the village to help them clear up.

The villagers may ask what she will do in the future. Options are to move down to the village; to bring her rubbish down, though it will be a difficult journey; or to bury food waste, burn paper and cardboard waste (being careful!), and to take bottles and tins to the recycling centre.

Sorting

Organise different types of material for recycling.

Recycling information

Collect posters and information from environmental bodies

Activity 6 Plenary in role

Teacher's intentions

- To encourage ordering of events when describing what has happened.
- To invite reflection on what has taken place and the implications.

Recalling the events: reflection

The villagers return to the Wise One to thank her for her help and to tell her about all their adventures. The teacher as the Wise One listens and asks questions where details need clarifying, such as which sorts of rubbish can be buried.

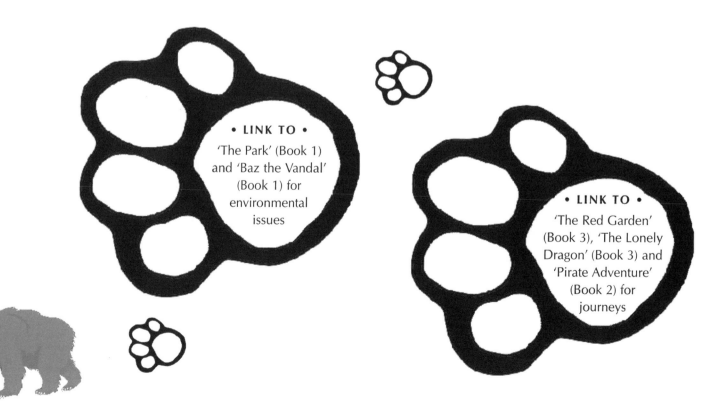

• LINK TO •
'The Park' (Book 1) and 'Baz the Vandal' (Book 1) for environmental issues

• LINK TO •
'The Red Garden' (Book 3), 'The Lonely Dragon' (Book 3) and 'Pirate Adventure' (Book 2) for journeys

CHAPTER 5

Goldilocks

Goldilocks is out looking for an adventure when she discovers a cottage with the front door open. It is owned by Mr and Mrs Bear and their son, Baby Bear. The bears have gone off for a walk while they wait for their porridge to cool. While they are away Goldilocks enters the cottage, tastes their porridge, breaks a chair and eventually falls asleep in Baby Bear's bed. What a surprise awaits the bears on their return!

Aims

- To explore a traditional tale.
- To use active storytelling approaches.
- To look at alternative viewpoints.

Themes

- Traditional story.
- Apologies.
- Right and wrong.

Resources

- Costume suggestions.
- A doll for Goldilocks to carry.

The imaginative play area can be designed as a cottage or a wood.

Goldilocks by Charlie

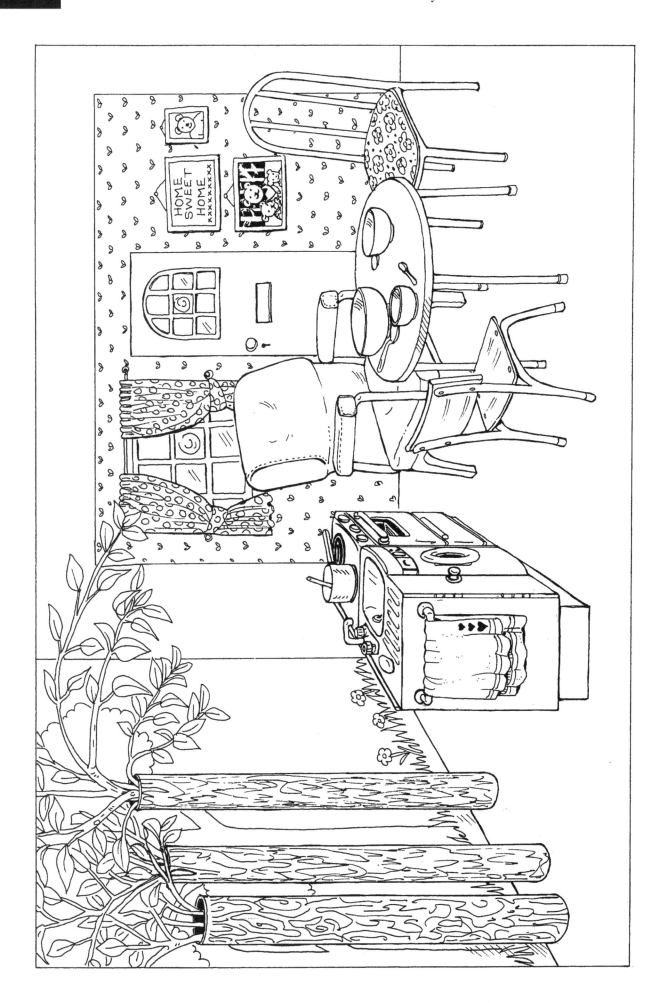

Activity 1   Meeting Goldilocks

Teacher's intentions

- To involve the children in storytelling.
- To introduce teacher in role as Goldilocks.
- To introduce questions concerning appropriate behaviour.

Shared storytelling: the beginning of the story

Tell the story leaving some gaps. The children fill in the gaps with words of their choice.

Once upon a time there was a little girl who was called Goldilocks. Everyone called her Goldilocks because she had such beautiful, long, golden ... [look at the children to supply the next word].

She lived in a small ... in the heart of a large .... One day, Goldilocks decided to go for a walk to a part of the wood she had not visited before. She took her ... and her ... and set off on an adventure.

Narration with mimed action: Goldilocks sets out on a walk

Ask the children to help to tell the story by acting out what happens as you tell it.

She walked slowly along the path, looking all around her as she went [walk around the room looking up and down].

She saw her friend the rabbit and waved happily at her as she hopped by [wave and say 'hello']. *Then Goldilocks began to skip along humming her favourite song 'Here We Go Round the Mulberry Bush'.* [All sing the song together.] *After a while she sat down on a log and had a rest. She was so sleepy in the sunshine that she fell asleep.*

A little while later, Goldilocks woke up and stretched. She looked around and saw a pretty cottage with a pink door and yellow spotted curtains at the windows. 'I wonder who lives in this cottage?' said Goldilocks, 'I'll just go and knock on the door.' When Goldilocks reached the door she saw that it was open. She knocked on the door and waited. 'Hello!' she called, 'Is there anyone at home?' No one answered.

Discussion in role: what did Goldilocks think she was doing?

- *What should Goldilocks do?*
- *We know that in the story she goes into the house when she shouldn't have.*
- *Why do you think she entered the house?*
- *What might she have expected? Was she hoping to find something?*

The children discuss questions they could ask Goldilocks, because they will soon meet her.

- *Why did you enter?*
- *Were you afraid?*
- *How would you feel if someone entered your house?*

© Jo Boulton and Judith Ackroyd (2004) *The Teddy Bears' Picnic and other stories*, David Fulton Publishers.

Story map

Journey to the bears' cottage. This can be made orally through telling the story of Goldilocks going through the wood. Alternatively, it could be told with drawings on large sheets of sugar paper or a white board.

Read and collect

Different versions of the story.

The children talk to teacher in role as Goldilocks. Play Goldilocks as naïve. She is not really sure what she has done wrong. The children need to help her understand.

- *The door was open, why shouldn't I go in?*
- *They should have locked the door if they didn't want anyone to go in.*
- *Why is it wrong to go into someone's house without permission?*
- *I didn't mean to get in trouble.*
- *I was bored.*
- *I was curious.*
- *I wondered who lived there.*
- *It looked so pretty.*
- *I could smell food and I was so hungry.*

Activity 2   Goldilocks tastes porridge

Teacher's intentions

- To move the story on.
- To invite the children to consider the implications of Goldilocks' actions.
- To change the narrator from third person to first person: Goldilocks.

Narration with mimed action: Goldilocks is hungry

Ask the children to join in the storytelling again by miming as though they are Goldilocks. It is Goldilocks who will tell the next part of the story.

Well, that was only the beginning. Do you know what I did next? I went into the kitchen. On the table were one, two, three [count and point] bowls of steaming porridge. I was so hungry [rub tummy], I just couldn't resist tasting that porridge.

First I tasted the porridge in the big bowl – it was too hot [mime tasting and reaction].

Next I tasted the porridge in the medium-sized bowl – it was too salty [again, with action and facial expression].

Then I tasted the porridge in the small bowl – it was just right. It was so delicious that I ate it all up. You would have done too wouldn't you?

Children may respond:

- *No we wouldn't.*
- *You were naughty.*
- *It wasn't yours.*
- *You were stealing.*

Goldilocks is confused:

- *But I don't understand.*
- *What does stealing mean?*
- *If it's just left there why can't I help myself?*
- *No one else seemed to want it. It was going to be wasted.*
- *I didn't know three bears lived here. I thought it was empty.*

Cooking/design and technology
Make porridge.

Setting the table
This may be done on a table to teach children how to set a table, or on sugar paper or a white board.

Narration: moving the story on

After she had eaten all the porridge in the small bowl, Goldilocks wanted to sit down. There were three chairs. She wondered why there were three of everything. She tried the big chair. It was too hard. She tried the medium-sized chair. It was too soft. She tried the small chair. It was just right. But Goldilocks was too heavy, and the chair collapsed and broke into hundreds of pieces. Then she went upstairs.

As she climbed she began to feel a bit strange. She began to worry that perhaps she wasn't supposed to be here.

Conscience alley: giving advice

The children stand in two lines facing each other. Move slowly down the line as Goldilocks. As you pass the children, each one tells her what they think of her behaviour or what she should do next. Examples:

- *You are a thief.*
- *Go home at once.*
- *How much will the chair cost to repair?*

At the end of the line, turn and announce, *I feel very tired now. I think I'll have a nap on this lovely comfortable tiny bed.*

Activity 3   The bears find Goldilocks

Teacher's intentions

- To invite consideration of Goldilocks' behaviour.
- To practise different facial expressions.
- To empathise with the bears.

Facial expressions: the bears see the porridge dishes

- *Invite the children to consider the relationship between facial expression and emotion.*
- *I wonder what happened when the bears came home from their walk?*
- *Imagine how the bears would feel when they returned. What do you think they would feel?* [children make suggestions]. *Curious? Surprised? Afraid?*

- *First they would see the porridge dishes.*
- *What sort of expression would Daddy Bear make when he saw the porridge dishes with two having been tasted and one completely empty?*

The children practise their expressions. Then divide the group into two halves. This enables each half to look at the others' expressions. They may say which they especially like and why, and what they think the expressions say about Daddy Bear's reaction.

Do the same with Mummy Bear's expression and then Baby Bear's expression when he sees his empty porridge dish.

Maths
Sets of three: small, medium-sized and large.

Art
Pictures of the three bears.

Gestures: the bears see the chairs

What would the bears do when they saw the chairs? The bears are so shocked that they cannot speak. But we can see what they felt by what they did.

Children can imagine which bear they are and decide what gesture they would make. They might put their hands to their heads, or step back with their mouths open. Children try out different gestures, and step back or forward to show what the bears might do.

Invite the children to show their gestures to the others.

Exclamations: the bears see Goldilocks

What would they think when they saw Goldilocks asleep in the bed?

The children think of exclamations, such as:

- *Get out of here!*
- *Help!*
- *Who are you?*

They experiment with their voices to create the effect they want: perhaps a confused bear, or a frightened bear. Volunteers voice their exclamations out loud for others to hear. Or all the children stand in a circle and take it in turns to step into the circle and make their exclamation before stepping back into the circle.

Do you know what she did? That's right, she ran home as fast as her legs would carry her.

Activity 4   Plenary

Teacher's intentions

● To reflect on the drama.
● To consider the implications of Goldilocks' action.

Meeting: the bears and Goldilocks

All of the children are in role as the bears. (It doesn't matter if there are three bears and thirty children!) Teacher is in role as Goldilocks. She may not be entirely sorry at first. She will respond to what the children say to her.

● *Mother has told me to come and say sorry to you.*
● *And I'm sorry I ate your porridge but I was so hungry. I thought it was going to waste.*
● *I'm sorry I broke your chair, I am so clumsy.*
● *I didn't realise that I was being naughty.*
● *What can I do to put things right? Can we be friends?*
● *Could you teach me how to make porridge?*

Discussion: what's been learned?

● What has Goldilocks learned?
● What must she remember not to do? Make a list
● What should the bears do when they go out?
● Does it make things OK now that she has said sorry?

> **Puppets**
> Retell the story using puppets. If you don't have glove puppets, try using teddies and a doll. We have used other objects as puppets, too, such as fluffy pencil cases for the bears and a smooth case for Goldilocks. The story takes over and the fact that you are using pencil cases becomes irrelevant.

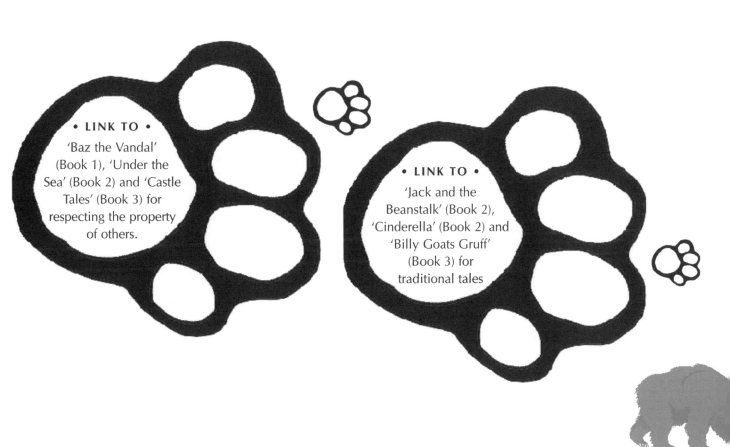

> • **LINK TO** •
> 'Baz the Vandal' (Book 1), 'Under the Sea' (Book 2) and 'Castle Tales' (Book 3) for respecting the property of others.

> • **LINK TO** •
> 'Jack and the Beanstalk' (Book 2), 'Cinderella' (Book 2) and 'Billy Goats Gruff' (Book 3) for traditional tales

6 Baz the Vandal

Everyone enjoys the park. Some enjoy it for their walks, others for the flowers, and children for the swings, slides and the twirling roundabout. Baz the Vandal likes to write his name on the slide and café wall in bright spray paint. The children meet with him to have a chat.

Aims

- To consider the social implications of graffiti.
- To create a context in which the children need to negotiate with an antisocial character.
- To evaluate the most appropriate way to produce a change in someone's behaviour.

Themes

- Care for the property of others and the environment.
- Different types of behaviour.
- Peer group pressure.

Resources

Optional: Aerosol paint spray can, baseball cap.

The imaginative play area can be organised using sheets or large pieces of sugar paper or wallpaper that children could spray paint to create 'street art'.

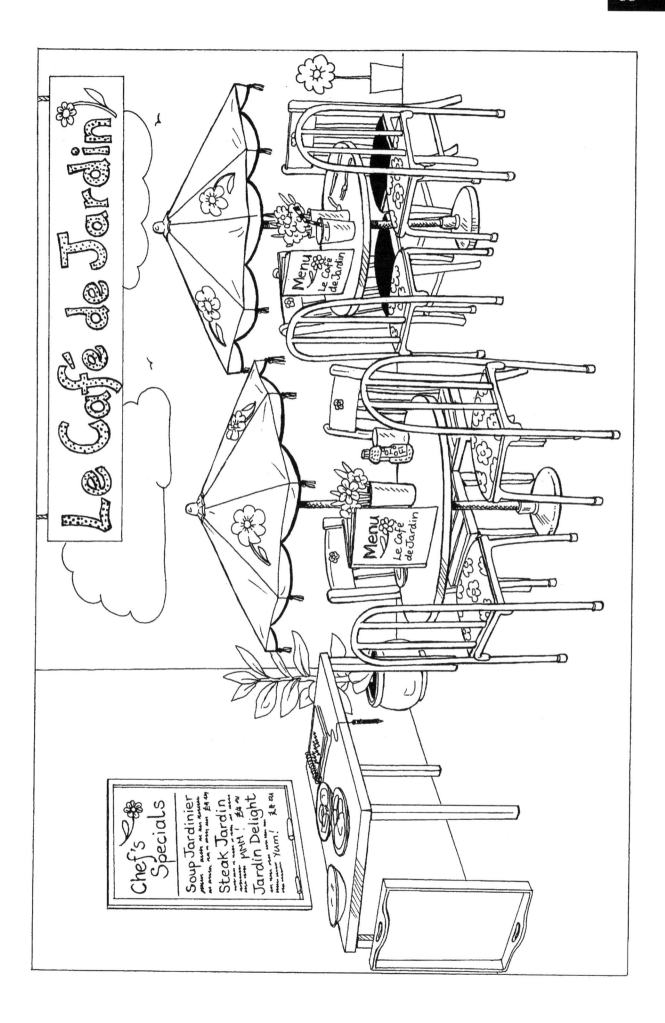

Graffiti wall

Paint names onto a roll of wallpaper.

Activity 1   Someone's out after dark

Teacher's intentions

● To introduce the graffiti.
● To consider views about graffiti.

Narration: One dark night . . . .

One dark night, when it was late and all the stars were shining down onto the park, a shadowy figure appeared from behind the café. It was a boy wearing a baseball cap and a jacket with the collar turned up. The boy crept along by the wall silently until he reached the children's slide. Suddenly, from inside his jacket, he produced a can of paint and began to spray a pattern all over the slide. It was a name. It said BAZ. He then did the same to the door of the café.

The next day, as people gathered in the park, they saw the name written on the slide and café door. They began to talk about it and to wonder what Mrs O'Connor would have to say. Mrs O'Connor worked in the café. They wondered whether the children would want to play on the slide today.

Discussion in role: what's going on in our park?

As one of those assembled in the park, instigate the conversation:

● *What on earth has happened here?*
● *Did anyone see anything?*
● *Why would someone do this to poor old Mrs O'Connor's café?*
● *What do you think the children will say when they come here today?*
● *What would we say if we caught someone doing this sort of thing?*

Design a park

What would you like to find in a park? Designs can be drawn individually, in groups or as a class sharing a large sheet of paper. Indicate play area, boating pond, cycle slopes, flower beds and so on.

Baz by Charlie

Activity 2   Meeting Baz

Teacher's intentions

- To use skills of argument and persuasion.
- To practise giving alternatives.
- To encourage listening to alternative viewpoints.

Statementing: who is Baz?

Ask the children to sit in a circle. Lay the baseball cap and spray can on the floor in the middle of the circle. Invite the children to think about what the owner of these items might be like.

Taking turns, the children speak one word or make a statement which describes what the owner of these items might be like (e.g. *He's very tough; scary; he has loads of friends*).

This activity may bring out stereotyped views which can be addressed when the teacher is in role as Baz.

Observation: Baz does his worst

Explain to the children that they can watch what happens the following evening.

Put on the cap and hold the spray can. Walk into the space, looking around furtively as if to see if anyone is watching you. Improvise actions as you speak.

There's no one about. They're all at home or out somewhere else. No one comes here at night.

No one will know it's me. I really enjoyed spraying my name last night. I fancy doing it again. Now where shall I spray this time? Hmmm...

Discussion: what shall we say to him?

Tell the children that they have a chance to challenge Baz and talk to him about what he has done. Practise a few questions that might be asked.

Tell the children that you will be Baz again and they will discover him in the park just before he sprays the café wall. Decide who will say the first words and what they will be (e.g. *What are you doing?*).

Whole-group improvisation: challenging Baz

Raise your arm as if to start spraying. The children challenge Baz. First he seems to think that it doesn't matter what they think as he's having a laugh and isn't thinking. He isn't thinking about how his actions are affecting others.

Examples of Baz's retorts:

- *I'm just having fun.*
- *I like doing this because it looks pretty.*

> **Character study**
>
> Draw a simple figure on a large sheet of paper. Even a stick figure would do. Invite the children to suggest words to describe Baz and write them around the figure. They could add words to describe him after the drama, when he has been persuaded not to be a vandal any more, in a different colour.

> **Poetry writing**
>
> Invite suggestions for single words that can be placed before 'Baz' to make up a list poem (e.g. Bad Baz; Daring Baz; Secretive Baz).
>
> The words in the poem may gradually change to describe the reformed Baz at the end of the poem (e.g. Guilty Baz; Sorry Baz).
>
> Prepare large sheets of paper with sprayed wavy lines. The children or teacher write the words of their poem within the spray lines.

Art

Use diffusers to create pictures using the colours of the park in a particular season. Groups could work with colours of the different seasons to depict all four seasons.

- *All my mates spray graffiti on walls so why shouldn't I?*
- *You can clean it off if you like but I'll just spray it again at night when you're at home.*
- *I don't really know Mrs O'Connor so it doesn't matter to me if she's upset.*
- *All my mates do it and I'd be weird if I didn't.*

The children may persuade Baz that his actions are unfair and suggest other options; for example:

- A special graffiti wall where they can all spray their names and create street art.
- Repainting Mrs O'Connor's café.
- Doing something more constructive.
- Not worrying about what his mates would say.
- Ignoring peer pressure.
- Spray painting the bins that have become very rusty.

Rap

'Baz the Vandal, in the park
Creeping out well after dark.
Sprayed his can and had lots of fun,
But others didn't care for what he'd done.'

The children can chant the rap with handclaps and/or percussion. They can add extra lines themselves.

Activity 3   Plenary

Teacher's intentions

- To consider the implications of one person's actions on others.
- To evaluate their suggestions to Baz.

Discussion: did we say the right things?

Talk about Baz and what they thought of him.

- *Was he a nice person?*
- *Why had he come to the park?*
- *Will he return to the park at night with his spray can?*
- *What did you help him to do?*
- *Did he change his mind?*
- *What did he like about the suggestions made?*

Retell the story of Baz in the park and predict what might happen in the future.

Shared writing
Write a list of rules for the park or a list of rules for the school playground.

Storyboard
The children or teacher draw storyboards to tell the story of the drama.

Discussion
What is right and wrong? Give children examples of social and antisocial behaviour and ask them to say whether they are 'right' or 'wrong' (e.g. dropping litter, putting litter into a bin).

Shared writing
With the teacher as scribe, the children write the diary that Baz may have written the night after meeting the children.

• LINK TO •
'The Dirty River' (Book 1), 'The Park' (Book 1) and 'The Road Garden' (Book 3) for environmental issues

• LINK TO •
'Goldilocks' (Book 1), 'The Lost Hat' (Book 1), 'Pirate Adventure' (Book 2) and 'Finders Keepers' (Book 3) for responsibility and respect for the property of others

7 The Health Centre

The new Health Centre is about to open after months of building work. New doctors who want jobs at the surgery are welcomed by Dr Molla who is in charge, and then they are shown around. Next, they have to undergo a short test to prove they are qualified for the job, and finally they are given an interview. All of the applicants are successful and start work in the busy surgery. There are some very interesting patients who come to the surgery for treatment.

Aims

- To share and use knowledge of doctors and health issues.
- To understand about the work of the doctor.
- To use appropriate medical vocabulary.
- To give advice and support to anxious people.

Themes

- Healthcare/doctors' surgeries/health centres.
- Giving advice.
- Caring for others.

Resources

Optional: large doll or rolled-up jumper to represent a baby.

The imaginative play area can be designed as the Health Centre.

The Surgery by Charlie

Resource

What's inside your body?

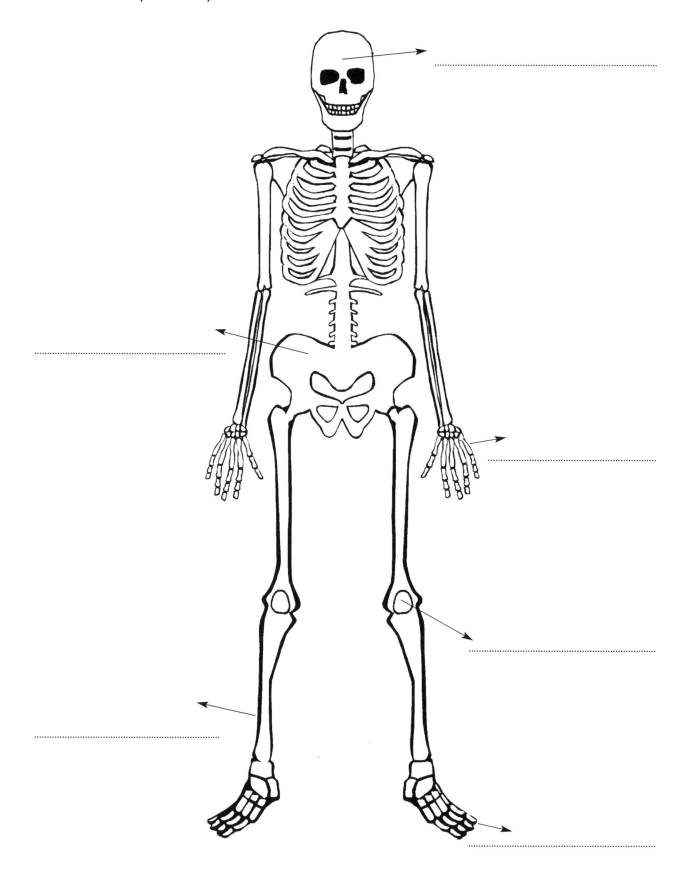

Activity 1   Meeting the new doctors

Teacher's intentions

- To introduce the teacher role and set the scene.
- To activate prior learning and knowledge about doctors.
- To build belief in the children's roles through role play.

Meeting: the doctor in charge greets the interviewees

Tell the children that they are going to be new doctors who want to work at the brand new Health Centre. They have come in today for an interview. What kind of training will they have had? Ask them to practise introducing themselves as 'Doctor'. This may be done in pairs or to the whole group. You are going to meet them at the door in role as the doctor in charge.

Good morning, everyone. I'm Dr Valerie Molla, the doctor in charge here. I've been a doctor for a long time now and I love putting plasters on broken legs and arms. I expect there are things you like doing best such as giving injections or looking after people with broken bones.

It's lovely to see you all here today for the interviews. We do have lots of new jobs here at the Health Centre and know you have all been working hard in your training to become doctors. First of all I'd like you to introduce yourselves and tell us what you like doing best as a doctor.

The children introduce themselves to Dr Molla. Ask questions to prompt contributions about giving medicine, sewing up cuts, giving injections and so on. Dr Molla mimes making notes about each 'applicant' as they introduce themselves.

Lovely to meet you all. Now we'll have a look around the building. Follow me.

Lead the doctors around the space, indicating the reception area, the cubicles, the medicine cupboard, the baby clinic area and so on. Ask the doctors questions such as:

Do you know how to put on bandages? What do you think we use this thermometer for?

Ask the children to sit down 'in the treatment room'. Choose a willing volunteer to come out to the front and 'pretend' to be a patient so you can demonstrate on them.

Good, now I'm going to demonstrate how we like things done here. I'm going to show you how to treat a patient who has come to see me with a nasty cough and cold. What equipment do you think I will need to use?

Examine the patient's ears and throat. Ask the children to advise you on the right equipment to use and the correct procedure to follow. Take the patient's temperature and ask to hear a cough. Prescribe some medicine if you like or give some good general advice about staying in bed and keeping warm.

Discussion

- Why do we need doctors?
- Where do we go to see the doctor?
- Who knows what a doctor's job is?
- When do we visit the doctor's surgery and when might we need to go to the hospital?
- Who is your doctor?
- What are doctors like? (Are they kind? Are they busy?)
- How does the doctor help the patient?

Make a list

Names of some medical equipment and terminology (e.g. stethoscope, prescription, syringe, medicine, plasters, bandages, injections).

Make

A name badge.

Dramatic play: testing patient care

It's now time for a little test to see how good you are at doing some of these things.

I'd like you to work with a partner. Now, one of you will pretend to be the patient who has come to the surgery with a graze on their knee or a bump on the head. You can choose. The other one will be the doctor who is going to clean up the graze and bandage the knee.

Children work in pairs to treat each other and give advice. Teacher in role monitors and makes suggestions.

This section of the drama can be as long or short as appropriate.

Discussion in role: what have you been doing?

Sit down 'for a tea-break'. Ask the doctors to describe what they have been doing.

The doctors are all given jobs at the Health Centre because they are so good!

Activity 2   The crying baby

Teacher's intentions

- To introduce a teacher in role who needs help and advice.
- To enable the children to sympathise with the teacher in role.
- To use appropriate language to encourage the role to talk.
- To use the children's collective knowledge of babies to offer advice.

Whole-group improvisation: what's wrong with the baby?

Tell the children that a man called Hugh has brought his baby daughter Carys to the baby clinic. He seems quite upset and wants to talk to someone about her. The doctors need to find out what is wrong. How will they speak to the man? What kinds of questions will they need to ask him?

The teacher can carry a rolled-up jumper or a large doll to represent the baby.

The children as doctors talk to teacher in role as Hugh. He sits holding his baby. He is not easy to talk to. He is reluctant to give much information, although he is clearly worried about the baby and holds it very lovingly and carefully in his arms. He doesn't want them to think that he is a bad parent. In fact he is a very good parent. The problem is that the baby is not sleeping at night and he and his partner can't get enough sleep. He is so tired.

What advice can the doctors give him? Hopefully, they will talk about things like singing lullabies, having a warm bath and cuddle before bed, and leaving a night-light on near the cot.

Hugh thanks them for their advice.

Safety advice
Importance of safe use of medicines.

Collective drawing
Draw an enlarged outline of a doctor's bag. Ask the children to think of what might be kept in the bag. Children come forward one at a time to draw an item onto the bag. The child or teacher can label the item and discuss its use.

Emergency services
Discuss what the emergency services are: Fire, ambulance or police and a coast guard for coastal regions and what they do. Using a play telephone, children dial and say 999. The teacher in role is the operator and asks: 'What service do you require?' Children take turns to be the caller in an emergency, giving the school's or their own address.

Activity 3   Plenary

Teacher's intentions

- To encourage reflection on what the children have done.
- To consider what has been learned about health centres and doctors' work.
- To invite connections between children's own experiences in life and the fictional centre.

Discussion: considering what has been learned

- The job of a doctor.
- The types of patients who might come to the surgery.
- The different examinations the doctors might do.
- The treatments given.
- The advice doctors might give.

These different roles and situations can be suggested to children to use in the imaginative play area on role cards. The children can take on these roles during free play sessions.

ICT

Appointment books; Prescriptions.

Singing games

Play 'Heads, shoulders knees and toes' game. Play the 'Hokey-cokey'.

Science

What's inside our body? Use the resource supplied on p. 60 to identify and name different parts of the body. The location of key organs such as the brain and the heart can also be pointed out.

Game for introducing medical terms

This game is played like Fruit Bowl, except with the names of items from the doctor's bag rather than fruit. So, the children sit in a circle on chairs. Each is allocated one of three names, e.g. thermometer, stethoscope or antibiotics. A caller in the middle calls out one of the names, e.g. antibiotics, and all the antibiotics have to leave their seats and find another to sit on. The caller's aim is to sit on a chair, too. Whoever is left without a chair is the caller in the middle. If 'Health Centre' is called, everyone has to leave their chairs and find another one.

• LINK TO •

'The Park' (Book 1), 'Not-So-Jolly Postman' (Book 1), 'Helping at the Pet Shop' (Book 2) and 'Farmer Roberts' Farm' (Book 2) for jobs in the community

• LINK TO •

'Teddy Bears' Picnic' (Book 1) and 'Baby Bunting' (Book 2) for caring for others

CHAPTER 8

The Park

Those who work in the park meet a number of different people who all have a different impact on them and on the park. Eileen, the café manager, is one of the workers, a real friend to everyone. The new path sweeper is called Tariq. He needs help to do his job. Mrs Strindberg from the local council threatens the jobs of those in the park, and even the park itself. Finally, those who work in the park meet Mr Khan who is rather lonely and has nowhere else to go every day. He is given a job in the park, and makes everyone smile.

A transcript of Activity 2 is provided on p. 9.

Aims

- To give the children the opportunity to practise talking to different people.
- To develop a sense of citizenship.
- To practise prediction.
- To interpret signs.

Themes

- Jobs.
- Public spaces: parks.

Resources

- At least two puppets of any type.

- *Costume suggestions*:
Eileen – apron, tea-towel, writing pad and paper.
Tariq – gardening clothes (old coat, wellington boots, hat, scarf, gloves), broom, ball of green string, black plastic sacks.
Mrs Strindberg – smart clothes, briefcase containing a large plan of the recycling centre.
Mr Khan – hat and coat (scruffy), bag containing puppets (not to be seen until the drama takes place).

The imaginative play area can be designed as the park.

Activity 1   Meeting Eileen

Teacher's intentions

- To establish the context of the drama.
- To enable the children to create their own place in the pretend world.
- To introduce the character of Eileen.

Narration: setting the scene

One sunny day in the park, all the people who were employed there were working very hard. Eileen, the lady who worked in the café, was going around the park and asking everyone what kind of sandwiches they wanted for their lunches.

Dramatic play: a routine day in the park

Explain that you will take the role of Eileen and ask the children to find a space in the room and go to 'work'. It is useful to wear an apron or carry a prop such as a tea-towel to indicate when you are in role.

As Eileen, walk around the park chatting to the workers and making a list of sandwich requirements. Minor incidents may arise (instigated by Eileen or as a natural result of the workers interacting in the park) (e.g. a lost dog; the mower runs out of petrol; it starts to rain).

Sharing stories: what we did at the park today

The children gather together and sit down. Discuss what has been happening in the park today.

- *What were you doing today?*
- *What kind of sandwich did you have for lunch?*
- *Did the dog do any damage?*

Activity 2   Meeting Tariq

Teacher's intentions

- To introduce simple costumes or props to build up an impression of the role.
- To provide the bag as a focus of interest and excitement.
- To develop the children's roles.
- To afford the children experience of giving advice through interacting with teacher in role.
- To give the children practice in describing and explaining.

Creating roles
Children decide what jobs they would like to do in the park (e.g. water the plants, sell ice-creams, cut the grass). Make a list of the jobs chosen.

Discussion
What do we know about parks? What might we find there? Make a list.

Collective drawing
Children draw an individual picture of something they would like to see in the park or of themselves working in the park. These can be stuck onto a large piece of paper to create a collective montage.

Still images

Jobs being done in the park. The children hold their positions to depict the job they are doing in the park while the teacher taps the children in turn and asks questions. Examples are: *What are you doing? What tools are you using? Is that tiring?*

Creation of teacher role: what's in the bag?

Place the bag of props in the middle of the circle of seated children.

Tell the children that in the story about the park they are going to meet someone new who has never been to the park before. This person owns the bag in the middle and they are going to find out more about this person by taking out one thing at a time and seeing if they can guess anything about the person who is going to visit them.

Invite the children one at a time to take things out of the bag and lay them on the floor. As each item of clothing or prop is removed, ask questions to draw out the children's understanding:

- *Who do think would wear a hat like this?*
- *Why are they carrying a ball of green string?*
- *What do we use a broom like this for?*
- *What is this?*

Tell the children that you are going to be the person who owns these things. Dress in the clothes and/or hold the props as appropriate. It's a good idea to give the person a name – we've called him Tariq.

The children go back into their spaces where they were doing their work as before. Tell them that the new person will be arriving soon and that they should look out for Tariq.

Whole-group improvisation: meeting Tariq

Go to the door and return slowly in role as Tariq. Perhaps develop a slight stoop and rub your back occasionally to give the impression that you are quite old and creaky.

Hello everyone. I'm looking for the park. Am I in the right place? Do you all work here?

Chat with the park workers. Tell them that you are the new path sweeper and haven't done this kind of work before. You need an outside job because of your asthma. Can they tell you what happens here and what you will have to do?

The children tell Tariq about the park and show him around. They may introduce him to everyone and show him where to find his tools and where to have a cup of tea.

Drawing or painting

A map of the park. Doing jobs.

Discussion: what did we make of Tariq?

Talk about Tariq and what they thought of him.

- *Was he a nice person?*
- *Why had he come to the park?*
- *What did you help him to do?*
- *How do you think he will get on with his job? Will he be good at it?*
- *Which words or phrases describe Tariq's impact on the park?*

Activity 3   Meeting Mrs Strindberg

Teacher's intentions

● To introduce a confrontational role.
● To encourage children to develop skills of persuasion and argue a case in role.

Creation of next teacher role: what's in this bag?

Place the new bag of props in the middle of the circle of seated children.

Tell the children that in the story about the park today, they are going to meet another person who has never been to the park before. This person owns the bag in the middle of the circle and they are going to find out more about the person by taking out one thing at a time and seeing what they can guess about who they are going to meet today.

As before, invite the children one at a time to take things out of the bag and lay them on the floor. As each item of clothing or prop is removed, ask questions to draw out the children's understanding.

● *Who do think would wear a hat like this?*
● *Why do people carry briefcases?*
● *Is this person smart, casual or scruffy?*

Whole-group improvisation: meeting Mrs Strindberg

Tell the children that in the story you are going to be the person who owns these things. Dress in the clothes or hold the props as appropriate.

Tell them that the new person will be arriving soon and that this time they are all having a tea-break in the café when the person arrives. Give children a minute to sit in the café and start handing out cups of tea.

Go over to the door and walk back smartly and purposefully. You smile very falsely at everyone and speak with a slightly superior tone. Mrs Strindberg is a slightly bossy and officious woman.

Good afternoon everyone. My name is Mrs Strindberg. I'm from the council. Are you all the people who work here in the park?

I need to have a chat with you about something very important. Can I sit down here? Good. Now then, I expect you've all heard that the council has been looking for a place to build a new recycling centre. People are so careful these days to recycle their cans and bottles, and the council wants to build a shiny new building where all the things can be brought. They have chosen this park as the best place to build the centre and I've brought the plans here today to show you.

Take the plans out of your briefcase and show them to the workers. By now they will be asking lots of questions and may even be shouting at Mrs Strindberg that it is not fair that their park has been chosen. Mrs Strindberg deals with this reaction by asking them for their ideas and saying she will report back to the council with their viewpoint.

Discussion: what did we make of Mrs Strindberg and her ideas?

● *What was Mrs Strindberg like?*
● *What was the council going to do?*
● *What could the workers do to stop the recycling centre being built in their park?*

Follow-up work to Mrs Strindberg's visit
Making posters: 'Save our Park'.
Writing a petition.
A newspaper article.
A television or radio interview.

Discussion
Who might suffer if the park was destroyed? Make a list.

Follow-up work to meeting Mr Khan

Make puppets and stage a puppet show.

Activity 4   Meeting Mr Khan

Teacher's intentions

- To encourage children to interact with a character in role who is lonely and miserable.
- To practise using supportive and encouraging language.
- To introduce an element of surprise when the bag of puppets is revealed.

Creation of final teacher role: what's in this bag?

Place the next bag of props in the middle of the circle of seated children.

Tell the children that they are going to meet a third person, who they have seen very often in the park, always sitting on the same bench and looking sad. This person owns the bag in the middle of the circle and they are going to find out more about the person by taking out one thing at a time, as before:

- *Who do think would wear a hat like this?*
- *Why do you think he looks so sad?*
- *Is this person smart or scruffy?*
- *I wonder what is inside this bag? Perhaps we'll find out when we meet the person who owns it.*

Tell the children that in the story you are going to be the person who owns these things. Dress in the clothes or hold the props as appropriate. Ask the children to give the person a name – we've called him Mr Khan.

Stories

Read stories about parks (e.g. *Percy the Park Keeper* by Nick Butterworth).

Whole-group improvisation: meeting Mr Khan

Tell the children that you will be Mr Khan and will be sitting on the bench in the park. The park workers have decided to speak to the man and find out why he looks so miserable and fed up. Decide what might be an opening line and ask for a volunteer to approach Mr Khan and begin the conversation.

Mr Khan responds in a very miserable voice, slowly giving out information:

- *I live alone.*
- *I come to the park every day to look at the birds and feed the ducks.*
- *I watch the children playing and remember when I used to work in this park many years ago.*

Hopefully the children will want to know what Mr Khan used to do. He was a puppeteer and put on puppet shows in the park for the children. He thinks that children these days are not interested in puppets and he hasn't done a show for years. With encouragement, he opens his secret bag to reveal a selection of puppets and does a show for the park workers. They may ask him to come again and do regular shows for the children.

Discussion: what do we make of Mr Khan?

Talk about Mr Khan and what the children thought of him.

- *Was he a nice person?*
- *Why had he come to the park?*
- *What did you do to help him?*

Story circle: ending the story of the park

Ask the children to sit in a circle and take it in turns to add a sentence to tell the story of what happens to the characters we have met in the park. You may provide some link sentences to keep the story going and to bring different parts together.

Activity 5　Plenary

Teacher's intentions

- To consider what has been learned about the people we have met in the park.

Discussion: comparing the characters

Encourage the children to compare the four characters they met in the park. How did each character change the atmosphere in the park? (e.g. Mrs Strindberg made them angry; Tariq made them happy).

Discussion
How did we feel about each of the different people we met? Make a list of words and phrases to describe them (e.g. Eileen – friendly, nice, happy; Tariq – nervous, needed help, had a bad back).

Storytelling
Retell the story of when Mrs Strindberg or Mr Khan came to the park.

Visit
Visit a park or look at pictures of different parks.

• LINK TO •
'Not-So-Jolly Postman' (Book 1), 'The Health Centre' (Book 1), 'The Park' (Book 1), 'Farmer Roberts' Farm' (Book 2) and 'Helping at the Pet Shop (Book 2) for jobs in the coummunity

• LINK TO •
'The Dirty River' (Book 1), 'Baz the Vandal' (Book 1) and 'The Red Garden' (Book 3) for environmental issues

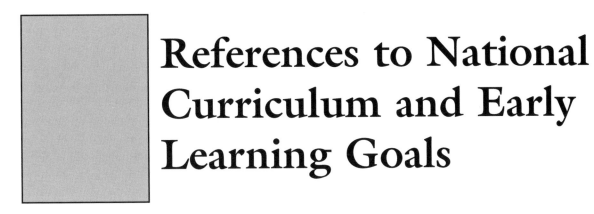

References to National Curriculum and Early Learning Goals

EARLY LEARNING GOALS

CHAPTER

EARLY LEARNING GOALS	1 Teddy	2 Postman	3 Lost Hat	4 Dirty River	5 Goldilocks	6 Baz	7 Health Centre	8 Park
Personal, social and emotional development								
1. Continue to be interested, excited and motivated to learn.	•	•	•	•	•	•	•	•
2. Be confident to try new activities, initiate ideas and speak in a familiar group.	•	•	•	•	•	•	•	•
3. Maintain attention, concentrate, and sit quietly when appropriate.	•	•	•	•	•	•	•	•
4. Respond to significant experiences, showing a range of feelings when appropriate.	•	•	•	•	•	•	•	•
5. Have a developing awareness of their own needs, views and feelings and be sensitive to the needs, views and feelings of others.	•	•	•	•	•	•	•	•
7. Form good relationships with adults and peers.	•	•	•	•	•	•	•	•
8. Work as part of a group or class, taking turns and sharing fairly, and understand that there need to be agreed values and codes of behaviour for groups of people, including adults and children, to work together harmoniously.	•	•	•	•	•	•	•	
9. Understand what is right, what is wrong, and why.	•	•	•	•	•	•	•	•
10. Consider the consequences of their words and actions for themselves and others.	•	•	•	•	•	•	•	•

CHAPTER

EARLY LEARNING GOALS

Communication, language and literacy

	1 Teddy	2 Postman	3 Lost Hat	4 Dirty River	5 Goldilocks	6 Baz	7 Health Centre	8 Park
1. Interact with others, negotiating plans and activities and taking turns in conversation.	•	•	•	•	•	•	•	•
2. Enjoy listening to and using spoken and written language, and readily turn to it in play and learning.	•	•	•	•	•	•	•	•
3. Listen with enjoyment, and respond to stories, songs and other music, rhymes and poems and make up stories songs, rhymes and poems.	•	•	•	•	•	•	•	•
4. Extend their vocabulary, exploring the meanings and sounds of new words.	•	•	•	•	•	•	•	•
5. Speak clearly and audibly with confidence and control, and show awareness of the listener, for example by their use of conventions such as greetings.	•	•	•	•	•	•	•	•
6. Use language to imagine and recreate roles and experiences.	•	•	•	•	•	•	•	•
7. Use talk to organise, sequence and clarify thinking, ideas, feelings and events.	•	•	•	•	•	•	•	•
12. Retell narratives in the correct sequence, drawing on language patterns of stories.	•	•	•	•	•	•	•	•
13. Show an understanding of the elements of stories, such as main character, sequence of events, and answer questions about where, who, why and when.	•	•	•	•	•	•	•	•

CHAPTER

EARLY LEARNING GOALS	1 Teddy	2 Postman	3 Lost Hat	4 Dirty River	5 Goldilocks	6 Baz	7 Health Centre	8 Park
Mathematical development								
1. Say number names in order in familiar contexts.		•						
2. Count reliably up to ten everyday objects.		•						
3. Recognise numbers one to nine.		•						
Knowledge and understanding								
4. Ask questions about why things happen and how things work.				•				•
9. Observe, find out and identify features in the place they live and the natural world.		•	•	•				•
Physical development								
1. Move with confidence, imagination and in safety.	•	•	•	•	•	•	•	•
2. Move with control and co-ordination.	•	•	•	•	•	•	•	•
4. Show awareness of space, of themselves and of others.	•	•	•	•	•	•	•	•
5. Recognise the importance of keeping healthy and those things which contribute to this.							•	
Creative development								
3. Use imagination in art and design, music, dance, imaginative and role play and stories.	•	•	•	•	•	•	•	•
5. Express and communicate ideas, thoughts and feelings by using imaginative role play and movement.	•	•	•	•	•	•	•	•

NATIONAL CURRICULUM OBJECTIVES

	CHAPTER							
	1 Teddy	2 Postman	3 Lost Hat	4 Dirty River	5 Goldilocks	6 Baz	7 Health Centre	8 Park
Key Stage 1 **En1 Speaking and Listening**								
Speaking								
1a speak clear diction and appropriate intonation	•	•	•	•	•	•	•	•
b choose words with precision	•	•	•	•	•	•	•	•
c organise what they say	•	•	•	•	•	•	•	•
d focus on the main points	•	•	•	•	•	•	•	•
e include relevant detail	•	•	•	•	•	•	•	•
f take into account the needs of the listener	•	•	•	•	•	•	•	•
Listening								
2a sustain concentration	•	•	•	•	•	•	•	•
b remember specific points that interest them	•	•	•	•	•	•	•	•
c make relevant comments	•	•	•	•	•	•	•	•
d listen to others' reactions	•	•	•	•	•	•	•	•
e ask questions to clarify their understanding	•	•	•	•	•	•	•	•
f identify and respond to sound patterns in language	•					•	•	

NATIONAL CURRICULUM OBJECTIVES	CHAPTER							
	1 Teddy	2 Postman	3 Lost Hat	4 Dirty River	5 Goldilocks	6 Baz	7 Health Centre	8 Park
Key Stage 1 **En1 Speaking and Listening**								
Group discussion and interaction								
3a take turns in speaking	•	•	•	•	•	•	•	•
b relate their contribution to what has gone before	•	•	•	•	•	•	•	•
c take different views into account	•	•	•	•	•	•	•	•
d extend their ideas in the light of discussion	•	•	•	•	•	•	•	•
e give reasons for opinions and actions	•	•	•	•	•	•	•	•
Drama								
4a use language and actions to explore and convey situations, characters and emotions	•	•	•	•	•	•	•	•
b create and sustain roles individually and when working with others	•	•	•	•	•	•	•	•
c comment constructively on drama they have watched or in which they have taken part	•	•	•	•	•	•	•	•
Language variation								
6a pupils should be taught how speech varies in different circumstances	•	•	•	•	•	•	•	•
b to take account of different listeners	•	•	•	•	•	•	•	•

NATIONAL CURRICULUM OBJECTIVES	CHAPTER							
	1 Teddy	2 Postman	3 Lost Hat	4 Dirty River	5 Goldilocks	6 Baz	7 Health Centre	8 Park
Mathematics **Key Stage 1** **Shape, space and measures**								
1a try different approaches and find ways of overcoming difficulties when solving shape and space problems		•		•				
b use correct language for shape, space and measures		•		•				
2a describe properties of shapes that they can see using the related vocabulary		•		•				
b observe and handle 2D shapes				•				
PSHE and Citizenship **Key Stage 1**								
1a to recognise what they like and dislike, what is fair and unfair, and what is right and wrong	•		•	•	•	•	•	•
b to share their opinions on things that matter to them and explain their views			•	•	•	•	•	•
c to recognise, name and deal with their feelings in a positive way			•	•	•	•		•
2a to take part in discussions with one other person and the whole class	•	•	•	•	•	•	•	•
c to recognise choices they can make, and to recognise the difference between right and wrong			•		•	•	•	•
d to agree and follow rules for their group and classroom, and to understand how rules help them	•	•	•	•		•	•	•

NATIONAL CURRICULUM OBJECTIVES

	CHAPTER							
	1 Teddy	2 Postman	3 Lost Hat	4 Dirty River	5 Goldilocks	6 Baz	7 Health Centre	8 Park

PSHE and Citizenship
Key Stage 1

Objective	1 Teddy	2 Postman	3 Lost Hat	4 Dirty River	5 Goldilocks	6 Baz	7 Health Centre	8 Park
e to recognise that people and other living things have needs, and that they have responsibilities to meet those needs	•	•	•	•	•		•	•
g what improves or harms their local, natural and built environments and some of the ways people look after them				•		•		•
3d the process of growing from young to old and how people's needs change							•	•
e the main parts of the body							•	
f that all household products, including medicine, can be harmful if not used properly							•	
4a to recognise how their behaviour affects other people	•	•	•	•	•	•	•	•
b to listen to other people, and play and work co-operatively	•	•	•	•	•	•	•	•
c to identify and respect the differences and similarities between people	•	•	•	•	•	•	•	•
d that family and friends should care for each other	•	•	•	•	•	•	•	•

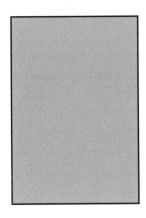

Glossary

This glossary of dramatic terms used in this book is not necessary to teach the activities in the chapters. Each activity is fully explained. However, a glossary providing explanations of a range of the dramatic approaches used in the book may help those who, having used them in these dramas, wish to plan their own drama sessions.

Conscience alley

This invites children to examine a moment in the drama in detail. It is employed most effectively when a decision has to be made, or when a decision has already been irrevocably made. Sometimes it also requires the children to offer advice to a character. Children consider what they or the character might think about the decision and its implications.

The children stand in two lines facing each other about a metre apart. The teacher walks very slowly from one end of the 'alley' to the other. As she does so, she turns to the child on one side and then on the other. They speak aloud a word or line (e.g. to Goldilocks, *You should leave this cottage*).

Discussion in role

Here the teacher and children are all in role while they discuss an issue or problem. The conversation is not *about* the characters (e.g. *What do you think frightens him?*) but *between* the characters (e.g. *Do you understand why I am frightened?*). The meeting takes place *as if* the teacher and children are other people in another place; in a fictional context. Discussion in role may be in the form of a formal meeting held to sort out problems or discuss plans.

Dramatic play

Here the children are involved in imaginative play, but in the context of the shared drama. They may be preparing some food, making a toy or painting a rocket. Although the action is initiated by the teacher, it is not controlled by her. The teacher may wander among the children asking them about what they are doing as though she, too, is involved in the fiction (e.g. *What flavour is your cake going to be? How will you make that? How did you reach to paint that top bit?*). The children have freedom for individual creativity, and to be involved in their own worlds, so that one is cooking a cake in a kitchen while another is shopping for drinks. High levels of concentration or emotion are not necessary in dramatic play, though of course they may occur. The activity helps to build up belief in the fiction.

Narration and narration with mimed action

Teacher narration in drama activities is often a very useful device to control the children's behaviour or the direction of a drama. The teacher is empowered to dictate particular aspects of the drama. A class working noisily, for example, may hear the teacher narrate, *Gradually, they fell silent. The helpers were too tired to speak.*

Narration is also used by the teacher to excite or build tension in the drama (e.g. *No one knew what was inside the bag. It might help them to solve their problems*). It can also be used to set the scene (e.g. *The hall was enormous and richly decorated*) and to move the action forward (e.g. *They all packed their bags and started the dangerous journey*).

We enjoy drawing the children into narration through mimed action (e.g. *The villagers had to climb up over high rocks* on a journey would be accompanied by everyone miming climbing over imaginary rocks). It may also be used to help the children to imagine they are all one character (e.g. *She put on her big strong boots, tying the laces tightly. She then put on a heavy coat and did up the buttons, one, two, three and four*). Each child, in his own space, will mime the actions as the teacher narrates.

Ritual

Ritual is a repeated procedure that those involved give value to and are familiar with. In drama a ritual is used to give action significance. Any action, no matter how mundane, may be performed in a formal and dignified manner to make the actions appear to matter. Putting items into a picnic basket, for example, by asking one child at a time to step forward and place an imaginary contribution into the basket announcing what it is, brings about a more serious level of thought to the action and a more exciting atmosphere. A ritual.

Statementing

Statementing involves the children literally in making statements about a person, event or place in the drama. The statements may be made in a ritualistic manner, with children stepping forward one at a time to say their statement. They may remain frozen in a gesture appropriate to the statement while others make their statements, or they may return to their original place and watch the others.

Still images and still image building

To make still images, children arrange themselves as though they are in a three-dimensional picture, depicting a scene or a particular moment. It creates a frozen moment when we imagine time has stopped, giving us the opportunity to look at it more closely.

Still images may be created by small groups, or by the whole group. They may be created quickly in the count to five, or they may be built one person at a time. This still image building approach enables children to respond to what others are doing in the still image by placing themselves in a position that relates to another's. A child seeing someone else in an image on a swing in a park may stand behind the swing as though she is pushing it higher.

Teacher in role

The teacher takes the role of someone in the drama. This enables the teacher to work with the children from inside the drama. Additional information may be given through the teacher's role and questions can be posed to challenge the children's ideas and assumptions.

Whole-group improvisation

This activity involves the children and the teacher working together in role. The teacher will have particular intentions in mind, but the ideas and suggestions offered by the children, and therefore the responses of the teacher, will vary when you work with different groups. It is this mode of activity that often generates a high level of concentration and emotional commitment. Unlike dramatic play, the children are all engaged in one world, dealing with the same problem.

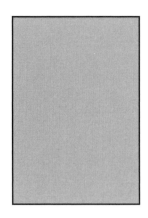

Suggestions for further reading

This is not a comprehensive list. There are many useful books available about drama in education and activities for the early years. We believe that the following books complement this series.

Ackroyd, J. (ed.) (2000) *Literacy Alive*, London: Hodder & Stoughton.

Ackroyd, J. and Boulton, J. (2001) *Drama Lessons for Five to Eleven-Year-Olds*, London: David Fulton.

Aldridge, M. (2003) *Meeting the Early Learning Goals through Role Play*, London: David Fulton.

Beetlestone, F. (1998) *Creative Children, Imaginative Teaching*, Buckingham: The Open University Press.

Bolton, G. (1984) *Drama as Education*, London: Longman.

Bolton, G. (1992) *New Perspectives on Classroom Drama*, London: Simon & Schuster Educational.

Booth, D. (1994) *Story Drama*, Markham: Pembroke.

Booth, D. (2002) *Even Hockey Players Read*, Markham: Pembroke.

Bowell, P. and Heap, B. (2001) *Planning Process Drama*, London: David Fulton.

Clipson-Boyles, S. (1999) *Drama in the Primary Classroom*, London: David Fulton.

Drake, J. (2003) *Organising Play in the Early Years*, London: David Fulton.

Emblen, V. and Helen, S. (1992) *Learning Through Story*, Leamington Spa: Scholastic.

Fleming, M. (1994) *Starting Drama Teaching*, London: David Fulton.

Kempe, A. and Holroyd, J. (2003) *Speaking, Listening and Drama*, London: David Fulton.

Miller, C. and Saxton, J. (2004) *Into the Story: Language in Action Through Drama*, New Hampshire: Heinemann.

Mudd, S. and Mason, H. (1993) *Tales for Topics: Linking favourite stories with popular topics for children aged five to nine*, Twickenham: Belair.

Neelands, J. (1992) *Learning Through Imagined Experience*, London: Hodder & Stoughton.

Neelands, J. and Goode, T. (2000) *Structuring Drama Work*, Second Edition, London: Hodder & Stoughton.

O'Neill, C. (1995) *Drama Worlds*, London: Heinemann.

Toye, N. and Prendiville, F. (2000) *Drama and Traditional Story for the Early Years*, London, Routledge Falmer.

Winston, J. (2000) *Drama, Literacy and Moral Education 5–11*, London: David Fulton.

Winston, J. and Tandy, M. (2002) *Beginning Drama 4–11*, Second Edition, London: David Fulton.

Ready, Steady, Play!

Guaranteed fun for children and practitioners alike, the Ready Steady Play! series provides lively and stimulating activities for children.

Each book focuses on one specific aspect of play offering clear and detailed guidance on how to plan and enjoy wonderful play experiences with minimum fuss and maximum success.

Each book in the Ready, Steady, Play! series includes advice on:

■ How to prepare the children and the play space

■ What equipment and materials are needed

■ How much time is needed to prepare and carry out the activity

■ How many staff required

■ How to communicate with parents and colleagues

Early years practitioners and students on early years courses and parents looking for simple, excellent ideas for creative play will love these books!

Available from September 2004!

Ready, Steady Play! helps you to:

■ Develop activities easily, using suggested guidelines

■ Ensure that health and safety issues are taken into account

■ Plan play that links to the early years curriculum

■ Broaden your understanding of early years issues

 David Fulton Publishers

Order Form

Qty	ISBN	Title	Price	Subtotal
	1-84312-148-4	Books, Stories and Puppets	£12.00	
	1-84312-098-4	Construction	£12.00	
	1-84312-076-3	Creativity	£12.00	
	1-84312-267-7	Displays and Interest Tables	£12.00	
	1-84312-101-8	Festivals	£12.00	
	1-84312-100-X	Food and Cooking	£12.00	
	1-84312-276-6	Music and Singing	£12.00	
	1-84312-114-X	Nature, Living and Growing	£12.00	
	1-84312-099-2	Play Using Natural Materials	£12.00	
	1-84312-147-6	Role Play	£12.00	
	1-84312-204-9	David Fulton 2004 catalogue	FREE	
			P&P	
			Total	

Postage and Packing: FREE to schools and LEAs. £2.50 for orders to private addresses. Prices and publication dates are subject to change

Please complete delivery details:

NAME: ....

ADDRESS: ....

....

POSTCODE: .... TEL: ....

EMAIL: ....

☐ **Please invoice** (applicable to schools, LEAs and other institutions). *Invoices will be sent from our distributor.*

☐ **I enclose a cheque** payable to *David Fulton Publishers Ltd.* (include postage & packing)

☐ **Please charge to my credit card** (we accept all major credit cards including switch).

Credit Card No:

☐☐☐☐☐☐☐☐☐☐☐☐☐☐☐☐

☐☐☐☐☐☐☐

Exp. Date: ☐☐☐☐

(Switch customers only)

Valid from: ☐☐☐☐ *Issue no:* ☐

FREE Postage and Packing to Schools and LEAs!

Send your order to: Harper Collins Publishers • Customer Service Centre • Westerhill Road • Bishopbriggs Glasgow • G64 2QT • Tel: 0870 787 1721 • Fax: 0870 787 1723 • www.fultonpublishers.co.uk

Please quote ref. DF0009 on your order